I0236399

Sermons and Addresses

on

Fundamentals

By LOUIS WESSEL

Concordia Seminary, Springfield, Ill.

SECOND EDITION

St. Louis, Mo.
CONCORDIA PUBLISHING HOUSE
1924

To the Christian Reader — Greeting!

The New Testament employs chiefly three terms to describe the activity of a Christian preacher. Each of these terms is found to be highly significant when examined as to its original meaning: the first indicates and delimits the preacher's authority; the second states the essential character of every message which he delivers; the third expresses the uniform aim and the intended effect of his preaching.

Preaching is, in the first place, discharging the functions of a herald, or ambassador. The preacher is the commissioned representative and spokesman of the Lord of lords and the King of kings. "If any man speak," namely, as a Christian preacher, says Peter, "let him speak as the oracles of God." 1 Pet. 4, 11. "Preach the Word," says Paul to Timothy, 2 Tim. 4, 2, namely, the Word which has been entrusted to him, the Word of God. Unmutilated and unchanged God's message must drop from the preacher's lips as it came out of the mouth of Jehovah. "For," says the last writer in the Bible, "I testify unto every man that heareth the words of the prophecy of this book, If any man shall add unto these things, God shall add unto him the plagues that are written in this book; and if any man shall take away from the words of the book of this prophecy, God shall take away his part out of the book of life, and out of the holy city, and from the things which are written in this book." Rev. 22, 18. 19. The first writer in the Bible has said the same things, Deut. 4, 2, and in the center of our Bible are found words of the same import, Prov. 30, 6.

This is serious business, very serious business. "He that hath My Word, let him speak My Word faithfully. What is the chaff to the wheat? saith the Lord. Is not My Word like as a fire? saith the Lord; and like a hammer that breaketh the rock in pieces? Therefore, behold, I am against the prophets, saith the Lord, that steal My words, every one from his neighbor. Behold, I am against the prophets, saith

the Lord, that use *their* tongues, and say, *He* saith." Jer. 23,
28—31. Paul, comparing the work of a preacher to that
of a mason, says: "According to the grace of God which is
given unto me, as a wise masterbuilder, I have laid the foundation, and another buildeth thereon. But let every man
take heed how he buildeth thereupon. For other foundation
can no man lay than that is laid, which is Jesus Christ.
Now, if any man build upon this foundation gold, silver,
precious stones, wood, hay, stubble; every man's work shall
be made manifest; for the day shall declare it, because it
shall be revealed by fire; and the fire shall try every man's
work of what sort it is. If any man's work abide which he
hath built thereupon, he shall receive a reward. If any
man's work shall be burned, he shall suffer loss; but he
himself shall be saved, yet so as by fire." 1 Cor. 3, 10—15.
God has marked those preachers as dangerous persons of
whom He says: "The Word is not in them." Jer. 5, 13.

Virtually, then, the preacher is a repeater: he speaks
what Another has said before him. He is a witness: he
declares not what he, but what Another has said or done.
He is an agent, or servant, sent upon an errand of his
Master. He is a channel through which water flows from
a fountain on high. He is a trumpet; and his sole care
must be that, when preaching, he give forth no "uncertain
sound." 1 Cor. 14, 8.

This does not by any means imply that preaching is
merely reciting Bible-passages. It is a known fact that
Scripture may be correctly quoted and incorrectly understood and applied. The object of speaking and writing is
to convey sense. Words are vehicles of thought, expressions of will. Their meaning is the important things. The
four letters *l-a-u-s* form a word both in the Latin and in
the German language, but the meaning is vastly different.
What the preacher really does when preaching the *Word* of
God is not to fill the ears of men with articulate sound,
but to convey to their minds the thought of God and
the will of God. He may use many words in doing this;
also words which are not found literally in the Scriptures:

he may take a Scripture-text apart to make his hearers see its full meaning; he may use a well-known term of his own choice to reproduce the meaning of a Bible-term. He is an expounder and interpreter of the Word of God by preaching it. And he applies the Word of God to individual persons and their particular needs. He shows the bearing which a general principle or rule has in a special instance. But in all this varied activity he is only "declaring all the counsel of God," Acts 20, 27, not anybody else's counsel, will, or thought, and therefore truly preaches the Word of God. Like a Bible translator he says in the vernacular of his hearers what God spoke originally in a foreign tongue. Like a jurist he shows the application of the statutes and ordinances of the Lord to all men and to all conditions. The Pharisees, scribes, and lawyers, in the days when Truth Incarnate spoke in their synagogs, prided themselves on having scrupulously guarded the very letter of the oracles of God, and were told that they had lost the substance of the divine truth by their interpretations of it and the traditions of their elders.

Pondering the view which the Bible takes of his vocation and life-work, when it calls him a herald, the preacher will feel both humbled and exalted. Humbled, because he must recognize that all the authority which he wields from his pulpit is borrowed and limited authority. He is nothing by himself while he is preaching, though he may be a sage, an artist, a saint in his personal aspects. If he were an angel from heaven and were to preach any other gospel than that which God has sent him to publish, God and men would have to curse him. Gal. 1, 9. There is no profession which requires such constant self-effacement as that of the Christian preacher. A herald betrays a trust reposed in him if he leads men to disregard and to neglect the message which he is come to announce, and, instead, to give themselves up to admiration of the speaker. The Christian preacher disappears in the tidings which he brings and is heartily content to disappear. Being a herald, he desires men to attend to *what* is being said, not to *who* is saying it or *how* it is being said. He is satisfied to be no more than the brass of the trumpet, the membrane of the cymbal, and leaves the glory of his message to the invisible Author thereof.

But what matchless authority is that of a human being who can come before his fellows and assert truthfully: "Thus saith the Lord"; "the Lord is in His holy temple: let all the earth keep silence before Him!" Hab. 2, 20. The consciousness of the grandeur of his delegated authority must, on the one hand, lift the preacher above the acclaim and admiration of the multitude: no man can honor him more signally than his Lord and Master has already honored him. On the other hand, it must elevate him above the sneers and frowns of an angry world to a position of sublime unconcern. What is the wrath of the rabble, the sarcasm of the wise, the scorn of the Caesars, the thunder of Antichrist, and the fury of hell to the good and faithful servant to whom his master says: Well done? Matt. 25, 23. If his authority is second-hand and circumscribed, his responsibility, too, is limited. He has delivered his message: that is sufficient. The message will take care of itself, and the Lord will take care of His messenger.

Preaching is, in the second place, proclaiming good tidings. In the Great Commission by which the departing Head of the Church authorized for all time preaching in all zones and climes, He employed a word which signifies telling a good tale, in Old English, a God's spell, a story so good that it can only come from Him from whom every good and perfect gift comes down to men. The earthly ministry of Christ was filled with the glory of many miracles, and He appealed to them occasionally to establish His identity as the Messiah. Matt. 11, 4 ff.; John 10, 37 f. But on one of these occasions, after recounting the splendid record of His signs and wonders, He asserted the highest criterion of His Messiahship in these words: "The poor have the Gospel preached to them." Matt. 11, 5. One of His first sermons of which the Bible has given a copious account — the one that He preached in His native village — is a Gospel-sermon from a text in Isaiah. On the basis of this text He declared it to be His mission "to heal the broken-hearted, to preach deliverance to the captives, and recovering of sight to the blind, to set at liberty them that are bruised, to preach the acceptable year of the Lord." Luke 4, 16 ff. To the end that the Gospel may be preached to all nations, He delays to-day His second coming. Matt. 24, 14.

The Gospel has to do with men in their fallen state of guilt and misery, helplessness and despair. To men who are feeling the lash of the accusing witness in their bosom, to whom hope has become a chimera, and comfort an unknown term, the Christian minister preaches Christ the Bearer of sin, the Atoner of guilt, the Conqueror of death and hell, the Harbinger of Heaven's peace and pardon. He teaches men to regard Christ as their Great Brother in His entire career on earth, who has repaired the damage of their iniquities, transgressions, and sins, who unintermittingly pleads their cause in His exalted state before the Judge of the whole earth, and who becomes in them, through His gracious Word, a quickening power, in which they go forth wrestling with their body of sin, with a world steeped in wickedness, and with the infernal legions. He is their righteousness before God, and in Him they achieve righteousness before men.

Before the preaching of the Gospel of Christ the pagan world of ancient times with all its glory of power, wisdom, and wealth went down to defeat. 1 John 5, 4 ff. In the shadow of His cross Christ proclaimed the world-conquering power of the Gospel of the Crucified, when He said: "And I, if I be lifted up from the earth, will draw all men unto Me." John 12, 32. In the era of the apostles, and in every age in which the Church has put forth her real strength, Christian preaching has been Christ-lifting and cross-lifting. It has been ringing with the appeal: "Look unto Me, and be ye saved, all the ends of the earth; for I am God, and there is none else." Is. 45, 22. Its spokesmen have been true paracletes; their messages have been the solace and cheer of men who sat pining amid the wreck of their hopes and aspirations, whose wisdom had been raised on fatal error, and whose ethics had been planted in a morass. To them the Gospel has opened up a new knowledge of things that "eye hath not seen, nor ear heard, neither have entered into the heart of man," 1 Cor. 2, 9, and a new source of "strength that is made perfect in weakness," 2 Cor. 12, 9.

But there has been such a thing as a "reproach of Christ," Heb. 11, 26, and ministers of the Church have ignobly surrendered the incomparable dignity of being purveyors and expounders of Christ's evangel, in order to seek distinction and influence by preaching the law of man's duties, morality, social reform. "They have forsaken the fountain of living waters, and hewed them out cisterns, broken cisterns, that can hold no water." Jer. 2, 12.

Because it preaches Christ, "who is made unto us wisdom, and righteousness, and sanctification, and redemption," 1 Cor. 1, 30, the Christian religion is distinct from every other religion, and an indispensable requisite of the Christian preacher is declared by Paul when he writes to Timothy: "Do the work of an evangelist"; for only thus can the Christian preacher "make full proof of his ministry," 2 Tim. 4, 5. If proclaiming the Gospel is one of the terms which the Scriptures employ for preaching, it follows that Christless preaching is not preaching in the Biblical sense.

Preaching is, in the third place, teaching. In the Great Commission the two terms "evangelizing" and "teaching" are correlated. By spreading the tidings of salvation the preacher becomes in a most effectual manner a teacher of men. Teaching presupposes ignorance and incapacity, and aims at information and equipment. The efficient teacher produces in his pupils both the ability to know and actual knowledge, and the ability to do and the actual doing of things. His sermons are for indoctrination and for energizing men unto the practise of their Christian profession. The Christian preacher is such a teacher. His sermons are storehouses of revealed knowledge, and attract attention for the reason that they are so very informing. They are powerhouses of the activity in which the life that is of God is exerted by a believer: they furnish the impulse, give the direction, and fix the aim for everything that the Christian thinks, speaks, and does. The Christian sermon thus becomes the school of faith: it equips men for a Christian character in the life that now is, and finally graduates them to the life that is to come.

The thoughts which I have just now expressed were suggested during the reading of the manuscript of my esteemed colleague's, Prof. L. Wessel's, collection of sermons and addresses which are offered to the Church in this book.

In a letter accompanying his manuscript the author says: —

"The sermons here presented were preached to a small country congregation which I serve. Besides discoursing on the Gospel- and Epistle-lessons for the church-year, I deemed it wise to preach on the principal doctrines of the Bible as presented in our Catechism. Instead, however, of making the text of the Catechism the foundation of the sermon and proving that statement from the Bible, I reversed the order. I selected a passage from the Catechism under a certain *locus,* endeavored to be led by it in the explanation and application, and at the same time tried to incorporate in the sermon the various truths suggested by the other Scripture-passages under said *locus.*

"This plan, of course, made an infringement upon homiletical rules necessary now and then. The purpose in view, the needs and circumstances of the congregation, however, seemed to justify the procedure.

"Some few discourses here presented have been thrown into a mold not generally countenanced by writers on homiletics. In order to present a certain doctrine entire in one address, *e. g.,* 'Christ Our King,' three or more passages have been utilized to set forth the main divisions of the doctrine consecutively. Having neither time nor inclination to recast these discourses, I give them as delivered.

"These SERMONS AND ADDRESSES were not originally written with a view to publication. Were it not for the fact of a dearth of Lutheran sermonic literature in English, a statement often made in our periodicals, and the remark just as frequently made that any contribution to such literature would be welcome, I could not have been moved to submit these discourses to the public, being fully aware of their shortcomings.

"It has been my earnest endeavor at all times by God's grace to preach 'Christ and Him crucified.' Him, my Savior and Redeemer, I would exalt. May God grant that this aim has been attained also in these SERMONS AND ADDRESSES! My prayer is that God may bless them to the salvation of souls."

I have been requested to introduce this book to the Christian reader, and I am happy to do this, now that the book goes forth upon its mission, by depositing my humble testimony to the effect that I have found the author conscious in every sermon which he submits in this volume of his character as herald, gospeler, and teacher. He comes to all who read this book on the King's business; he brings with him the Balm of Gilead; he instructs us unto faith and godliness. He has honored his Lord and his profession by this publication; may the Lord bless his printed message abundantly as He blessed the spoken message to those who heard it!

W. H. T. DAU.

Concordia Seminary, St. Louis, Mo.
April 25, 1918.

PUBLISHERS' NOTE.

The remarkable success attained by this book is a source of gratification to the publishers as well as it should be a source of real satisfaction to the author.

This volume of sermons never really was intended for the general public; and the fact that we nevertheless sold out the entire edition in six years is therefore a safe indication that the professional trade found this collection distinctly serviceable.

THE PUBLISHERS.

CONTENTS.

The Follies of the Fool that Denies the Existence of God.

ROM. 1, 18—20.

For the wrath of God is revealed from heaven against all ungodliness and unrighteousness of men who hold the truth in unrighteousness. Because that which may be known of God is manifest in them; for God hath showed it unto them. For the invisible things of Him from the creation of the world are clearly seen, being understood by the things that are made, even His eternal power and Godhead, so that they are without excuse.

"The fool hath said in his heart, There is no God." He who maintains that there is no God is a fool, a wicked, a godless person. Such fools to-day call themselves atheists. In the days of the psalmist they were not outspoken in their foolishness. Timidly they said in their hearts, "There is no God." To-day, figuratively speaking, they proclaim their unbelief from the housetops. And this they believe to be great wisdom. But what does Scripture say? "Professing themselves to be wise, they became fools." "Fools," godless, wicked persons, that is the Scripture name, God's designation of such people as deny the existence of God. Their stupendous folly becomes manifest from a consideration of our text. In accordance with the text and under the guidance of the Holy Spirit let us treat of

The Follies of the Fool that Denies the Existence of God.

> *1. He stifles the voice of his conscience.*
> *2. He denies the evidence of his senses.*

1.

St. Paul, in our text, speaks of people on whom as yet the Holy Ghost has not operated through the Word, of heathen, of unbelievers. He says it is a grievous sin that they do not use their natural knowledge of God, and he proves them to be without excuse, that is to say, it is their own fault that the wrath of God will finally destroy them to the uttermost. They have a capacity to know that there is a God, and that this God is their Judge. "God left not Himself without witness." Acts 14, 17.

But let us follow the trend of the apostle's thoughts. — *"The wrath of God is revealed from heaven against all ungodliness,"* that is to say, all sins against the First Table, *"and unrighteousness,"* all sins against the Second Table. When he says: "The wrath of God is revealed," we may think of the Flood, of the confusion of tongues, and similar manifestations of God's wrath against sin, but the Last Great Day, as we know, will preeminently be a day when His wrath will be revealed *"from heaven,"* from the seat of His majesty. It will be a wrath that none can evade, though they invoke the hills to cover them and the mountains to fall upon them.

What does the apostle say of these people against whom God's wrath is, and shall be, revealed? What is the sin they commit? They are *"men who hold the truth in unrighteousness."* What is this "truth"? As the context proves, it is the truth which all nature loudly proclaims: "There is a God." This truth they "hold down," *i. e.,* they suppress, they stifle it. They know this truth, but, behold their folly, they hold it down forcibly! The natural knowledge of God demands recognition, it forces itself, as it were, upon men. Their conscience testifies to this fact, but they will not listen to this language. Why this foolish attitude? The apostle answers this question by saying they hold this truth down, suppress it, *"by unrighteousness."* They are unrighteous people, people who revel in sin, who will not quit sin, who love sin. But since there is a God, as their conscience tells them, they know that this God will one day punish them for their evil-doings, that this God is their Judge, — and then woe unto them! So they try to calm their troubled conscience by denying the existence of God.

How unspeakably foolish! The ostrich, we are told, when pursued, burrows his head in the sand, believing the pursuers will not see him because he cannot see them. The infidel knows a day of reckoning is sure to come; so his conscience, the God-given voice within him, tells him. What does he do? He smothers this voice by denying the existence of God, as though by that act he could dethrone God. Ah! the love for "unrighteousness," for sin, for wallowing in the mire, only too often is the cause of man's denial of the existence of God. Loudly the unbeliever mouths his unbelief — in daylight; but in the wee small hours of the sleepless night conscience speaks a different language. In a terrible catastrophe, such as the shipwreck of the *Titanic* of recent date, or an earthquake, such as the one in California some years ago, — where is your atheist? Wringing his hands, his face is upturned to heaven for deliverance to that God whose very existence he had denied but a few hours ago.

Said a minister to one of these pitiable wretches who boldly proclaimed his unbelief: "See here, there are three classes of people who deny the existence of God. The first class are those who profess to have reasoned the thing out scientifically. You are not a man of science, so you do not belong to this class, do you?" "No." "The second class is made up of babblers, who speak as they do because they have heard some 'great man' say these things. Do you belong to this class?" "No, of course not." "Well, there is but one class left, and this is composed of men who live in sin and shame, who have a seared conscience and are afraid of God, their Judge, who will one day speak with them in His wrath. Since you do not belong to the first class and not to the second, you must belong to this third class." The man was silenced.

Indeed, the wrath of God will be revealed against all "who hold the truth in unrighteousness." The fault is man's. It is not ignorance on his part; he is not excusable. Hence the wrath of God is just. How great is the folly of the fool who strangles the voice of his conscience! But that is not all. This fool also denies the evidence of his senses.

2.

"Because that which may be known of God is manifest in them; for God hath showed it unto them. For the invisible things of Him from the creation of the world are clearly seen, being understood by the things that are made, even His eternal power and Godhead."

Let us follow the text closely. *"That which may be known of God is manifest in them."* The apostle says: There are certain things of God that are knowable to natural man; these things are "manifest *in them*," in their minds; they know them. How do we know them? *"For God hath showed it unto them."* Which are these things? The apostle says they are the *"invisible things of God."* Which are they? *"His eternal power and Godhead,"* the divine attributes of the Deity. Man knows there is a God, almighty, eternal, all-wise, benevolent. What does the apostle say of God's eternal power and Godhead? They are "invisible." Though these attributes are invisible, still they are *"clearly seen."* How are they clearly seen? *"Being understood"* — by the intellect, by the understanding. How can the intellect clearly see God's eternal power and divinity? From the works of creation. The text

says: *"Being understood by the things that are made."*
Natural man, seeing the works of creation, can understand,
clearly see, the divine attributes of God, such as His power,
eternity, and wisdom; hence he can know that there is
a God, that this world must have had a Maker.

You observe the seeming contradiction: "The *invisible*
things of God are *clearly seen.*" How can we see invisible things? Let me endeavor to clear up this matter
somewhat. There are two classes of things in this world:
things perceived by the five senses and things perceived
by the intellect, by reason, by the understanding. How
do I learn about a house? I see it, hence I know it exists.
How do I learn about music? I cannot see it, I cannot
smell it, I cannot taste it, but still it exists. How do
I know? I hear it. So we learn of various things by
means of the five senses; of the one thing by this sense,
of another thing by another. But there are some things
about which we cannot learn anything by means of the
senses, and still they exist. There are such things as pride,
wisdom, anger. Can we see pride, wisdom, or anger? No.
Still these things are knowable. We see the manifestations
of pride, anger, and wisdom, and thus learn about these
unseeable things. When you observe a person strutting
along the streets grandly conscious of his importance and
dignity, you say: There goes a proud person; he is possessed with pride. But this abstract quality — pride —
you cannot see; you learn of it through the intellect.
Just so it is with this dictum of the apostle: *"The invisible things of God"* — His eternal power and divine
attributes — *"are clearly seen,"* not, indeed, with the eye,
but with the understanding, as St. Paul explicitly adds:
"being understood." How does reason learn of these
things? *"By the things that are made."* Man, says the
apostle, seeing the works of creation, will understand, his
reason must tell him, that there is a First Cause, a Maker

of these things, who, though invisible, has manifested Himself, His power and divinity, through His wonderful works.

And since when has God so manifested Himself? *"From the creation of the world."* As long as there was and is a creation, so long God's attributes have been seen and still are seen. When we see an article labeled, "Made in Germany," we assume it really to have been made in that country; and when we look at the marvelous works of nature, we see the inscription written across the skies: "Made by the hands of God." In contemplating the world, the thought forces itself upon one: What a marvelous power that must have been to produce this universe! And so God's power is seen. Still further reflection would impel one to say: This power which called the world into existence must have been prior to all created things; it must have been eternal. And thus God's *eternal* power is seen, and by viewing the wonderful order, harmony, adaptability, etc., in creation, one would be driven to acknowledge God's wisdom and benevolence.

And now, what does he do who denies the existence of God? He denies the evidence of his senses, of his reason, that thing upon which he prides himself so much, and thus falls to the level of brutes. Brutes see the sun, the moon, the stars, but they do not see the hand of God back of them. Why? They are brutes, irrational beings. Man, however, when seeing these visible things, is at the same time capable of seeing the invisible, God's eternal power and divinity, not with the eye, but with the mind. This is the meaning of that acute saying: "The invisible things are clearly seen." And a man who does not use his reason here is foolish.

A noted French astronomer of the last century (Lalande, † 1837) is said to have pointed his telescope to the heavens and, not seeing God, to have asserted, "There is no God!" That was foolish. He used a wrong method of finding

God. That reasoning of his was just as nonsensical as though one were to say: There is no music, for I cannot see it; there is no sun, no moon, there are no stars, because I cannot hear or smell them. That act of the infidel astronomer was just as nonsensical as was that of the little boy who wanted to find out where the sweet song of the singing bird was secreted. He killed the bird, but he did not find the song.

To learn about the existence of God, one must use the right method, and that, says the apostle, is by means of the intellect. God is knowable, not by means of the eye and the telescope, but by means of the mind. The invisible things of God, His power, His wisdom, His benevolence, are clearly seen by the works of creation. These works of creation speak an unmistakable language, a language so plain that the ditch-digger as well as the philosopher can understand it and is constrained to confess: There must have been a Maker of the universe. And this Maker, or Creator, we call God.

Athanasius Kirchner, a famous German astronomer, a devout Christian, had a friend who doubted the existence of God. One day this man paid Kirchner a visit. The astronomer was busy, and so his friend looked about the room. A beautiful globe attracted his attention. He asked Kirchner whether the globe belonged to him, who had made it, etc. Kirchner replied that it did not belong to him, that he did not know where it had come from, that nobody had made it, and that it must have gotten into his study of its own accord. His friend at first thought that Kirchner was merely jesting, but when the latter repeated his statements with apparent seriousness, he became vexed and reproached Kirchner for making sport of him. "Well," said Kirchner, "see here: you refuse to believe that this little miniature globe came into existence of its own accord and still you profess to believe that the great world itself has no Creator. Don't you see how foolish you are?" The unbeliever was silenced.

St. Paul's dictum, *"God has showed it to them,"* *i. e.,* that there is a God, needs no proof. It is God's Word. But do you require further assurance? Go to heathen lands, and you will find that the inhabitants, however degraded they may be, possess the knowledge of the existence of a god, whom they worship in one way or the other in order to gain his favor or to appease his anger. Cicero wrote a treatise *On the Nature of the Gods.* He made a bungling job of it, but he proved that there is a God. Aristotle, another noted heathen thinker of ancient times, says: "God, who is invisible to every mortal being, is seen by His works."

And now, friends, behold the follies of the fool who denies the existence of God. He *"holds down the truth by unrighteousness"* and thus renders himself *"without excuse."* He smothers the voice of his conscience, and thus he is without excuse. *"The invisible things of God are clearly seen from the works of creation,"* but he discards the evidence of his own senses, and thus he is without excuse. The heathen nations, the ancient and the modern world, loudly testify to the truth of Paul's assertion, but he turns a deaf ear to their testimony, and thus he is without excuse. God's wrath will be revealed against him. His damnation is just.

There is a God — this every honest person must admit. But with only this natural knowledge of God, man is but a heathen. This knowledge does not make him a Christian. It does not teach him who the true God is, and how He is minded towards him. God, of whose existence we learn through the works of creation, has revealed Himself in the Scriptures. From these alone we obtain a saving knowledge of God; from them we learn that the true God is triune — God the Father, God the Son, and God the Holy Ghost. We learn, furthermore, that out of love to this sin-stricken world God gave His only-begotten Son to redeem it from sin and damnation, and that every one that believeth on the Son as His Savior shall not perish, but have everlasting life.

Thank God, my Christian friends, that you have been brought to a knowledge of the truth as it is in Christ Jesus, our Lord, blessed forever! Amen.

The Origin of the Holy Scriptures.

2 TIM. 3, 14—17.

But abide thou in the things thou hast learned and been assured of, knowing of whom thou hast learned them, and that from a child thou hast known the Holy Scriptures, which are able to make thee wise unto salvation through faith which is in Christ Jesus. All Scripture is given by inspiration of God and is profitable for doctrine, for reproof, for correction, for instruction in righteousness, that the man of God may be perfect, throughly furnished unto all good works.

It becomes necessary from time to time to speak about the Bible. You know that the devil is always busy through his emissaries, the enemies of Christianity, to discredit Holy Writ, God's Book. To timid Christians these attacks seem formidable, especially if made with pomp and a great blare of trumpets. To such, however, as are acquainted with the tactics of the enemies and the utter futility of their attempts, their proceeding would be amusing, were it not for the deplorable fact that these assaults cause some weak Christians to doubt the divinity of Scripture and thus to lose faith.

The Bible cannot be destroyed; it is God's Book. For

nineteen long centuries a terrific warfare has been waged against it, but all in vain. During the first three centuries of the Christian era the devil summoned up all his wit and ingenuity to do away with this Book, but failed. The genius of man, the philosophy of man, the science of man, the satire of man, was brought to bear against it, but all ended in failure. Next, the military and the political power of the old world made war against it — but all in vain. Edicts were issued by powerful emperors to burn all the Scriptures, thus to root out this new religion — that failed. Orders were issued to burn the Christians who owned Bibles and thus to uproot Christianity — and that failed. The blood of the martyrs became the seed of the Church. Then, later on, under the *régime* of the Pope, the people were forbidden to read the Bible — that failed. Anything, everything, was tried to discredit the Bible's teaching or to suppress it — but still the Bible stands unscathed.

And in our own times — well, the devil remains the devil — the warfare is still going on. The devil has simply changed his tactics. Years ago in Germany, the cradle of the Reformation, a school of criticism arose which taught and still teaches: This and that in the Bible is not true. The devil is trying the same old ruse that worked so well with Eve in the Garden: "Yea, hath God said?" This so-called "new learning," made in Germany, has been transplanted to our shores and is being peddled in most of our American universities. But now this "new learning," too, is on its deathbed, but the Bible still stands.

The devil, however, will not rest. It is the old story: One school of criticism under the veil of great learning arises and fails; another arises and fails, and still other enemies will try again. And the Bible? Why it still stands! As one writer remarks: "A Book that has successfully withstood nineteen centuries of assault of the devil's heaviest artillery is not going down before the air-guns of modern criticism." What saith the Lord? "Heaven and earth shall pass away, but My words shall not pass away."

But though the Bible is indestructible, still, since we live in these perilous, seductive times, it behooves us to learn anew from time to time of the priceless treasure we possess in the Bible.

The best antidote for the poison of the revilers of the Bible is a study of the Bible itself. Thus all doubts vanish as the mist before the sun's morning rays. Observe what Paul says to Timothy. In the verses preceding our text the apostle warned Timothy against errorists and de-ceivers, "against evil men and impostors who wax worse and worse, deceiving and being deceived." These and their evil ways he is to shun. *"But abide thou in the things thou hast learned and hast been assured of, knowing of whom thou hast learned them."* Thou hast learned the Christian apostolic doctrine from me, Timothy; and I have received it not from men, but from Jesus Christ Himself; hence it is divine doctrine. Furthermore, *"from a child thou hast known the Holy Scriptures,"* i.e., the sacred writings of the Old Testament. Your mother, Eunice, taught you these, and so did your grandmother, Lois, while you were a mere child, aye, a babe. And now, Timothy, grown man that thou art, thou knowest that what thou hast learned in thy youth from the Old Testa-ment is corroborated by what you have been taught by me, and I have been taught by Christ. Of this thou art assured; hence abide in these things. — Now, what is true of Timothy applies also to us. Hence I appeal to you: *Abide by the Holy Scriptures, 1. because of their origin; 2. because of their properties; 3. because of their purpose.*

This evening we shall speak of

The Origin of the Holy Scriptures.

"All Scripture," says Paul, *"is given by inspiration of God."* The apostle here speaks preeminently of the Scriptures of the Old Testament. But what is true of the Old Testament is equally true of the New, as we shall presently see. "All Scripture is given by inspiration of God." That says plainly: God is the Author of the Scriptures. He gave them. How? *"By inspiration."* "Inspiration," inspire, means "to breathe into"; "all Scripture is given by inspiration of God," in plain English, therefore, means: "All Scripture is God-breathed." Now, God is a spirit; hence this breathing was not a physical act, but a breathing of the Spirit of God. The Scriptures are God's work, God's words, God's sentences, God's thoughts; the Book is God's Book.

A God-breathed Book, a unique Book, indeed! All the countless millions of books in the world are but the productions of fallible men; many of them worthless, some positively harmful, most of them replete with errors, none perfect, the best of them standing in need of revision soon after publication, many becoming obsolete; but here is one Book that has no faults, cannot err, cannot become obsolete, is always fresh, always new and up to date, because it is God-breathed. "Given by inspiration of God," God-breathed — what a stupendous assertion! Assert this of man's books, of Shakespeare's works, Milton's, Longfellow's — say they are God-breathed, and you shudder. The very thought is a sacrilege. But Paul here in the most matter-of-fact way, without fearing resentment or contradiction, says: "All Scripture is God-breathed." Paul himself was one of the holy men of whom Peter says: "They spake, moved by the Holy Ghost." And here is such an utterance which he was moved to speak and write: "All

Scripture is given by inspiration of God." All Scripture
is God-breathed.

"God-breathed," what does that mean? It speaks of
the origin of the Bible. God did not drop these books down
from heaven as a fixed quantity, nor did He write the
words with His own finger as He did once upon a time
the Ten Commandments upon tables of stone on Mount
Sinai. He spoke through the mouths of His holy prophets,
as Peter informs us. Acts 3, 21. "Holy men of God
spake as they were moved by the Holy Ghost." 2 Pet.
1, 21. In some peculiar, unmistakable way they were
moved, driven, impelled, to write. Thoughts came to them
not latent in them before; the impulse to write came, and
write they did, not things of their former knowledge;
thoughts, glorious, grand thoughts, thoughts of God for
the salvation of man. And during the writing they were
filled with wonderment at the things of God they were
writing, and after completing the writing, they studied
and restudied their own writings for a deeper knowledge
of the things God had breathed into their minds and pens.
So says Peter: "Of which salvation the prophets have
inquired and searched diligently, who prophesied of the
grace that should come unto you, searching what or what
manner of time the Spirit of Christ, which was in them,
did signify, when He testified beforehand the sufferings
of Christ and the glory that should follow." 1 Pet. 1,
10. 11. This, briefly, is what is meant by this wonderful,
mysterious act of God — inspiration.

To acquire a fuller perception of what this means,
read your Bible. Everywhere it teaches that it is inspired,
God-breathed. In the five books of Moses expressions such
as these occur hundreds of times: "Thus saith the Lord";
"the Lord said"; "the Lord spake." Turning to the
prophetical books, we hear the prophets saying again and

again: "Hear the word of the Lord"; "the word of the Lord came to me." Everywhere not man speaks, but God.

Turning to the New Testament, we find that it gives testimony to the Old. Matthew time and again uses phrases similar to this: "Now all this was done that it might be fulfilled which was spoken of the Lord by the prophet." Matt. 1, 22. The Lord God is the Speaker; the prophet is but His mouthpiece. The apostles numberless times bear testimony to the Scriptures of the Old Testament as being God's Word. Jesus Himself gives testimony to the Old Testament to the same effect. In the great temptation in the wilderness He said to the devil: "It is written! It is written!" Again: "Till heaven and earth pass, one jot or one tittle shall in no wise pass from the Law till all be fulfilled"; "Have ye not read in the Law," etc.; "Moses wrote of Me," and similar expressions.

And as to the New Testament. On the day of Pentecost, we read, "the disciples were all filled with the Holy Ghost," who thus made them the infallible teachers of all mankind. Everywhere, too, in the New Testament the word that we read is the Word of God. To the Thessalonians Paul writes: "When ye received the Word of God which ye heard of us, ye received it, not as the word of men, but, as it is in truth, the Word of God, which effectually worketh also in you that believe." 1 Thess. 2, 13. Thus in almost countless instances it is asserted that the Scriptures are God-breathed. Explicitly the Apostle Paul teaches that even the choice of words was not left to the option of the holy writers, but that the Holy Ghost supplied them. He says, 1 Cor. 2, 13: "Which things also we speak, not in the words which man's wisdom teacheth, but which the Holy Ghost teacheth"; and in Gal. 3, 16 he bases an argument regarding the Messiah on the singular form of a word used in the Old Testament. He says: "Now, to

Abraham and his Seed were the promises made. He saith not, And to *seeds,* as of many; but as of *one,* And to thy Seed, which is Christ."

Hence, such sentiments as these: "The thoughts in the Bible are God's thoughts; the words are man's words," are utterly false. Thoughts depend upon words; if the words are not God-breathed, the thoughts cannot be. So, then, away with such nonsense!

But do you mean to say that all the Bible says is true, *e. g.,* historical and astronomical data, the account given of the creation of the world, etc.? Exactly. The first page of the Bible is God-breathed as well as the second or the tenth. If we cannot give credence to these earthly things recorded in the Bible, how, then, could we believe when it speaks of heavenly things? In short, the whole Bible, from cover to cover, is true. God cannot err. And let it be said right here that all arguments of the unbelievers have been met time and again before you and I were born. And to-day? There is nothing new under the sun. But be it also said, our faith in the Scriptures does not rest on our ability, or that of others, to answer these critics, but upon the Scriptures themselves. "Thy Word is truth." The topic: The origin of the Holy Scriptures, is a vast one; we are loath to close, but we must not overtax your patience.

Paul admonishes Timothy: "Abide thou in the things thou hast learned and been assured of, knowing of whom thou hast learned them." As Timothy knew of whom he had learned, and was fully assured of the divine origin of the Scriptures, so we, too, by the Word itself, by the witness of the Holy Spirit in our hearts, are fully convinced that this Book is God's Book. With Timothy of old we will, by God's grace, abide in the things we have learned. The sentiments and experiences of our hearts we clothe in

Peter's words, who, when the Lord asked His disciples: "Will ye also go away?" answered: "Lord, to whom shall we go? Thou hast the words of eternal life. And we believe and are sure that Thou art that Christ, the Son of the living God." Amen.

The Properties of the Bible.

2 Tim. 3, 15—17.

And that from a child thou hast known the Holy Scriptures, which are able to make thee wise unto salvation through faith which is in Christ Jesus. All Scripture is given by inspiration of God and is profitable for doctrine, for reproof, for correction, for instruction in righteousness, that the man of God may be perfect, throughly furnished unto all good works.

When we ask people of other denominations, "Do you believe the doctrine of your Church to be the true doctrine?" the answer generally is, "Why, of course." When, however, we question further, "Why do you assume your doctrine to be the true doctrine?" the answers vary. The papist says: "Our doctrine is true because it is the doctrine of the Roman Catholic Church, whose head is the Pope. In matters of faith and ethics he cannot err. Whatsoever the Pope demands of us to believe, that we believe. We get our doctrine from the Pope through the priest. In other words, I believe what the Church believes, and the Church believes what I believe. The Roman Catholic Church is the repository of truth; if she should decree a new dogma to-day, we Catholics would be obliged to accept it."

Before the year 1854 Catholics believed that Mary, the mother of our Lord, was conceived and born in sin. But because Pope Pius IX in that year announced the dogma of the immaculate conception and birth of the Virgin, Catholics have since then been forced to believe that. Prior

to 1870 Catholics believed that the Pope, being a fallible
man, could err also in matters of faith and religion; in
1870, however, the infallibility of the Pope was decreed;
now, therefore, they must accept that decree as divine truth
under pain of excommunication.

When we propound the question to members of various
Protestant denominations: "How do you know your doctrine to be the truth?" some say: "Well, we find that our
doctrine agrees with our enlightened reason and our Christian experience." Others say: "We have an immediate,
divine revelation, an inner light, certifying us as to the
truth of our religion." Still others evasively answer:
"We accept the principal doctrines of the Bible, to which
all Christian denominations agree, while as to the rest, in
which there are differences of opinion among the various
church-bodies, we are liberal enough to allow every one to
believe whatsoever suits him best."

We Lutherans, however, answer the question, "How do
you know the doctrines of the Lutheran Church to be true?"
thus: "We know our doctrine to be true because it is
founded on the Word of God and fully agrees with it.
Our motto is: 'Thy Word is Truth.' John 17, 17. God
cannot lie, neither can He err, nor can His Word err. The
Bible is the *only source* of all Christian truth. The Bible
is so *clear* that every one who can read may learn the truth.
The Bible is the *all-sufficient source* of truth and faith,
so that all that is necessary to salvation is contained
therein; and, finally, it is also the *powerful means* to
generate faith in man's heart."

These are the principal properties of the Bible. These

Properties of the Bible

we shall briefly consider to-day.

St. Paul says: *"All Scripture is given by inspiration
of God and is profitable for doctrine, for reproof, for*

correction, for instruction in righteousness." "All Scripture" is God's Scripture, God's Word. All words of this Book are backed by *God's authority* — all words, whether of the Law or of the Gospel.

The Bible issues commands to all. It says, "Thou shalt," and, "Thou shalt not." It is no respecter of persons: be they emperors, kings, princes, presidents; be they dressed in silk or satin, or in home-spun garments; be they parents, husbands, wives, children — to all alike it says, "Thou shalt," and, "Thou shalt not." It assumes authority over all men. God says: "And ye shall observe to do all the statutes and judgments which I set before you this day." Deut. 12, 32. And again Scripture says: "To the Law and to the testimony! If they speak not according to this Word, it is because there is no light in them." Is. 8, 20.

"All Scripture is profitable for doctrine," that says: If you want to know what "doctrine," teaching, God's teaching, is, you can find it nowhere else than in this Book. It alone speaks authoritatively on this matter. Whatever has no Scripture warrant is false doctrine, cannot claim divine authority, but is vain worship. Christ says of the Pharisees: "In vain they do worship Me, teaching for doctrines the commandments of men."

To-day, as all wide-awake Christians know, there is a determined effort in some quarters to set aside the authority of the Bible. We have read a series of sermons under the caption, "The Religion of the Modern Man," by a so-called minister of the Gospel, in which he flatters his hearers by calling them "modern men," for whom, of course, the religion of their forbears is out of date. But we "modern men," so this preacher asserts, accept and believe what we think to be right and good; our reason is the arbiter of matters of faith and life. Live a virtuous life and do things worth while for the community in which you live.

That is the new creed; thus you will be saved. It is not primarily what Christ did for you, but what you do for yourself and others, that counts. — Thus Christ is simply a pattern after whom you are to copy your life. All this in the name of "science" and "scholarship" and "the democratic spirit of the age."

How well St. Paul, or rather, the Holy Spirit, knew how to fortify the Christians against such vain babblers! Our text, this eulogy of the Scripture, is based upon the very statement that "perilous times" would come, endangering the soul; that "deceivers" would arise, who would endeavor to cause men to forsake the old faith. Therefore, says St. Paul, "abide by the Scriptures," abide by their inspiration, their authority. So he admonishes Timothy, so he admonishes us. And what does God say through His prophet Isaiah? "To the Law and to the testimony! If they speak not according to this Word, it is because there is no light in them." And to the Galatians, St. Paul thunders these words: "But though we or an angel from heaven preach any other gospel unto you than that which we have preached unto you, let him be accursed." Oh, that we could imprint this truth with indelible letters on the tablets of our hearts: "All Scripture is given by inspiration of God" and therefore is God's authoritative Word, given for our salvation!

And because it is God's Word, it is *all-sufficient*. This is another property of the Bible we would briefly consider. Paul says: All Scripture is *"able to make us wise unto salvation";* that is, it contains everything necessary to reach the goal — salvation. We need no other books, precepts, promises, revelations, or what not, to supplement the Bible-teachings. The Catholics are wrong in saying that the Bible is not sufficient unto salvation and in speaking so highly of the traditions of the Church handed down from generation to generation. This is simply a ruse on their part to pat the Bible on the back and call it a good book, and, at the same time, to set aside the Scriptures whenever convenient. When speaking in public to Protestants through their Jesuit missionaries, they endeavor to make them believe that they think highly of the Scriptures. They quote it as the devil quoted Scripture for his own purpose, and distort it, as did the devil, for his purpose. The traditions of their Church, the decrees of a fallible Pope, are their rule and guide. What Christ says of the traditions of the elders applies with equal force to the traditions of the Pope — they make the Word of God of none effect. The Bible, and it alone, as the text says, is "able to make wise unto salvation, that the man of God may be perfect, throughly furnished unto all good works."

The Pope and the Scriptures never agree. The Bible is all-sufficient for salvation. It is never to be superseded by traditions, nor by so-called Christian Science, nor by Mormonism, nor by "new revelations" of any kind purporting to be from God. All such doctrines are twaddle. Timothy, abide thou by the Holy Scriptures!

The story of the rich man and Lazarus is very instructive here. The rich man went to hell because he despised "Moses and the prophets," the Word of God. In hell he turned, as we would say to-day, to Spiritualism. He requests Abraham to send Lazarus to his five brethren to convert them, lest they, too, come to this place of torment. Abraham says no. "Let them hear Moses and the prophets." The rich man remonstrates: "Nay, Father Abraham, but if one went to them from the dead, they will repent," whereupon Abraham makes answer: "If they hear not Moses and the prophets, neither will they be persuaded though one rose from the dead." Luke 16, 29 ff.

But not only is Scripture the sole authority in matters

of faith, not only is it the all-sufficient guide to heaven, but it is furthermore *so clear, so perspicuous,* in teaching the way to salvation that even a child can understand it.

This is another property of Scripture to which we wish to call your attention. St. Paul says to Timothy: "And that *from a child* thou hast known the Holy Scriptures, which are able to make thee wise unto salvation." As you know, Timothy's mother, Eunice, and his grandmother, Lois, instructed the young child in the Scriptures. The plan of salvation is so simple, so clear, that the child understood it perfectly, and through the Word believed it, so that the apostle can truthfully say of Timothy: From a child you were made wise unto salvation by faith which is in Christ Jesus.

Again you see that the Catholics are wrong in maintaining that the Bible is obscure and, hence, in forbidding the reading of it by the laity. Once more the Catholics and the Bible do not agree. The psalmist says: "Thy Word is a lamp unto my feet and a light unto my path," and again: "How shall a young man cleanse his way? By taking heed thereto according to Thy Word." "Search the Scriptures," says Jesus Himself; "for in them ye think ye have eternal life, and they are they which testify of Me."

But the Bible possesses still another property: this we call its *efficacy,* its *power;* that is to say, it is itself the powerful instrument to bring about the purpose for which it was inspired — to save man. Let us hear the words once more: "From a child thou hast known the Holy Scriptures, which are *able* to make thee wise unto salvation." Man cannot make himself wise unto salvation. The ability to do so inheres in the Scriptures. The power of the Word does not depend on the preacher's oratory or eloquence, but the power is in the Word itself. Why? Because it is *God's* Word. God's power is in and with this Word. Hence St. Paul says to the Romans: "I am not ashamed of the Gospel of Christ, for it is a *power of God* unto salvation." God's Word is spirit and is life. Hence St. Peter says that it is a "living Word," a Word that has life and imparts life. Bringing this Word to the people, we bring the Holy Spirit, the power of God, to the people. Give this Word but a chance at the sinner's heart, let but this Word be spoken to the people, and it will manifest its power to save. Paul spoke the words of the Lord to the Philippian jailer "and to all that were in that house," and the jailer "rejoiced, believing in God with all his house." Acts 16, 23. Lydia, a seller of purple, heard Paul preach the Gospel, "and the Lord opened her heart that she attended unto the things which were spoken of Paul." Acts 16, 14. On that memorable first Pentecost Day, Peter preached the Word, and three thousand souls were added to the Church. God's Word needs not the embellishment of human arts. It is not a thing that must be preached with human aids "to make it go," but it is the eternal truth, a two-edged sword, powerful, living, and life-giving. It has the power to enlighten the sin-darkened mind of natural man, to break down all stubborn opposition of man's natural heart, causing it to see Jesus as the only Savior from sin.

But I must close. We have learned from the text what a precious Book the Bible is. Let us not be led astray by false prophets, who would rob us of this priceless treasure.

Thank God, we have experienced its saving power. Let us diligently search the Scriptures. This is an admonition we all need. Why is it that many know so little of its power and sweetness? Is it because the Word has lost these qualities in the course of the centuries? No! It is as powerful and sweet to-day as it ever was. The fault is ours. We do not read diligently and regularly in our

homes; we frequently neglect the preaching of the Word.
Can a medicine prove its power when it is not used? The
more, however, we read God's Word, the more we become
convinced of its authority, its sufficiency, its clearness, its
power, and the more we love it. We experience the truth
of the Psalmist's words: "How sweet are Thy words unto
my taste! yea, sweeter than honey to my mouth."
Ps. 119, 103. The more we study the Word, the stronger
our faith will become, and the more we shall learn to say
confidently in spite of all gainsayers: "I know whom I have
believed and am persuaded that He is able to keep that
which I have committed unto Him against that day."
2 Tim. 1, 12. Amen.

The Purpose of the Holy Scriptures.

2 Tim. 3, 15—17.

And that from a child thou hast known the Holy Scriptures,
which are able to make thee wise unto salvation through faith
which is in Christ Jesus. All Scripture is given by inspiration
of God and is profitable for doctrine, for reproof, for correction,
for instruction in righteousness, that the man of God may be
perfect, throughly furnished unto all good works.

This passage contains St. Paul's classic eulogy on the
Holy Scriptures. It consists mainly of three parts: the
origin, the properties, and the purpose of the Scriptures.
In a previous sermon we considered the origin of the Bible
and learned that it is "given by inspiration of God." The
Lutheran Church teaches a plenary verbal inspiration,
i. e., that the whole Bible from beginning to end is God's
Word; that the very words are God-inspired. Though we
could not consider all arguments, still we have seen how
well fortified this doctrine of inspiration is. In another
sermon we dwelt upon the properties of Holy Scriptures:

the authority it wields over all men, its all-sufficiency, its clearness, and its power to save. To-day, by God's grace, we shall consider

The Purpose of the Holy Scriptures.

This purpose Paul expresses thus: *"From a child thou hast known the Holy Scriptures, which are able to make thee wise unto salvation through faith which is in Christ Jesus."*

So the purpose of the Scriptures is to *make* man *wise,* to teach wisdom, true wisdom, the highest wisdom attainable. There is a countless number of books in this world, and they all have one purpose in view: to make man wise — wise in history, in science, in art, and what not. And how men glory in this wisdom, how they boast of it! Oftentimes, however, it is but a very questionable wisdom. But granted that the wisdom learned from these books is good in itself, it is merely for this life and at best helps to promote one's temporal welfare.

Holy Scripture, however, is a book in a class all by itself. It teaches a wisdom which reason could not attempt to teach because it knows nothing thereof; it teaches wisdom *unto salvation.* Suppose you possessed all the knowledge this world can offer; it would last but for a season; you must die. "What shall it profit a man if he gain the whole world and lose his own soul?" Here is a problem in profit and loss: Gain the world, lose the soul; what is the profit? How high, therefore, is the purpose of this God-given Book: to make wise unto salvation, to gain the soul! And this is the only purpose for which this Book was given. Upon this fact St. Paul lays all stress in our text: "Holy Scriptures are able to make wise unto salvation." Everything in the Bible, from Genesis to Revelation, has some connection with this grand object — "to make wise unto salvation." How sublime the purpose!

How insignificant in comparison with it are the purposes and contents of all other books! When the apostle says: "The Holy Scriptures are able to make wise unto salvation," he means to say: Without them there would and could be no true knowledge of salvation; they, and they alone, can make wise unto salvation; without them all mankind must remain in utter darkness as to the all-important question, "What must I do to be saved?" For by nature we are ignorant of things spiritual, however wise we may be in matters mundane. By nature we all live in the valley of the shadow of death without any light to dispel the darkness, without any knowledge of the way of peace. There is but one Book that can speak with authority on this subject, and that is the Bible, because it is God-breathed.

And what does it teach as the wisdom unto salvation? *"Faith in Christ Jesus."* "And that from a child thou hast known the Holy Scriptures, which are able to make thee wise unto salvation *through faith which is in Christ Jesus."* Natural man, left to his own imagination, thinks he can appease God by observing this, that, or the other thing; by offering sacrifices, by works of his own devising. Such was the idea of ancient heathenism; and modern heathenism has not surpassed it. Modern heathenism, oftentimes under the garb of Christianity, says: A virtuous life, an upright moral character, is the essence of Christianity. Boiled down, ancient and modern heathenism teaches that by his own works and merits man can earn salvation.

Scripture is diametrically opposed to this. "By the works of the Law shall no flesh be justified." Again, "As many as are of the works of the Law are under the curse." The only way to attain salvation is "by faith which is in Christ Jesus." "Oh, I see," says the scoffer, "all you need to do is to say, 'I believe,' and live as you please." Wrong, my friend! You know not what sin is nor what grace is; you have not the faintest idea of either the Law or the Gospel. The way to salvation is "by faith in Christ Jesus." So says St. Paul. Who is Jesus? The Savior; that is what this name "Jesus" means. So to believe in Jesus means to believe in Him as your Savior. That, however, presupposes your need of a Savior. That, again, presupposes the knowledge that you are lost without Him; otherwise you would need no Savior. For Christ came into the world to save that which was lost. Lost! — how? By sin. For no other purpose did Christ become man than to save sinners, "to save His people from their sins." Through the fall of our first parents the whole world was sin-lost. Sin separated God from man. "Your iniquities," says Isaiah, "have separated between you and your God." To be a sinner, then, means to be separated from God, to be damned. God created man good, righteous, holy. Voluntarily man transgressed the Law of his Maker. God is a righteous, a just God. He cannot suffer man to transgress His Law with impunity. His verdict is: "Cursed is every one that continueth not in all things which are written in the book of the Law to do them." That is the death-knell of us all. For "all have sinned and come short of the glory of God." David pleads: "Enter not into judgment with Thy servant, for in Thy sight shall no man living be justified." "We are all as an unclean thing, and all our righteousnesses are as filthy rags," Isaiah confesses. We are sinners, damned sinners. "The soul that sinneth, it shall die." — Where is help to be found? Nowhere in the world; not in us. Lost! But behold the boundless love of God! He devised a plan of salvation. The Law, the expression of His holy will, must be fulfilled. We could not do it, and therefore, "when the fulness of the time was come, God sent forth His Son, made of a woman, made under the Law, to redeem them that were under the Law, that we might receive the adoption of sons." "God hath made Him to be sin for us who knew no sin that we might be made the righteousness of God in Him." Now, whosoever believes in Christ Jesus possesses the righteousness that avails before God; upon him God looks as though he had fulfilled all the commandments himself. "Christ is the end of the Law to every one that believeth." Thus faith in Christ Jesus saves; thus faith in Christ Jesus is the only wisdom unto salvation. "There is no condemnation to them which are in Christ Jesus."

And when the apostle says: "All Scripture is given by inspiration of God and is profitable for doctrine, for reproof, for correction, for instruction in righteousness," he means to say: Because the Scriptures are "God-breathed," therefore they are profitable for these things. And these things: doctrine, reproof, etc., all tend to the same thing: to make wise unto salvation and to keep man on the way to salvation. "All Scripture is God-breathed," God speaks in the Scripture; hence the *doctrine* taught here is the only saving doctrine, the essence of which is salvation by faith in Christ Jesus. Of all doctrines not taught in the Bible our Lord says: "In vain they do worship Me, teaching for doctrines the commandments of men." Scripture is profitable for doctrine, hence we should prayerfully read it to become all the more sure of our salvation. But man is a sinner, and his sinfulness and the error of his ways must be shown to him. This Scripture does. It is profitable for *reproof.* Sinners must learn to amend their evil ways. This, too, Scripture teaches: it is profitable for *correction.* The sinner who has learned to know Jesus as his Savior is now eager to run the way of God's commandments, to follow after sanctification; and for this, too, Scripture is profitable, for it instructs in *righteousness.* Thus we see that all that Scripture teaches has one object in view: to make wise unto salvation, *i. e.,* to lead man to a true knowledge of his sin, but, above all, to make him know his Savior and to kindle faith in Him, to instruct him to walk in the way of righteousness after he has accepted Christ, and to keep him thereon in faith unto his blessed end.

And now as you read your Bibles, you will find this to be true from the first Gospel-promise in Genesis 3 to the last page in Revelation. Everywhere in the Old as well as in the New Testament the central theme is: Salvation by faith in Christ Jesus. Job, in view of death, exultingly exclaims: "I know that my Redeemer liveth." Old Simeon, with the Christ-child in his arms, says: "Now lettest Thou Thy servant depart in peace; for mine eyes have seen Thy salvation." The keeper of the prison, anxiously inquiring, "What must I do to be saved?" is told, "Believe on the Lord Jesus Christ, and thou shalt be saved." Peter exclaims: "There is none other name under heaven given among men whereby we must be saved" but that of Jesus. And St. John asserts that his entire Gospel was written but for this one purpose, "that ye might believe that Jesus is the Christ, the Son of God, and that, believing, ye may have life through His name."

Oh, what a blessed purpose the Scriptures have! Abide by the Holy Scriptures, Timothy! They are "able to make thee wise unto salvation." This admonition is also for us: "Hold that fast which thou hast that no man take thy crown." We know that we have passed from death unto life; we know in whom we have believed, and that God is able to keep that which we have committed unto Him against that day. Hence, by God's grace, let us abide by the Holy Scriptures. And let us thank God that we belong to the Lutheran Church, which teaches this wisdom unto salvation in all its purity, truth, and directness. Amen.

What Does Christ Say of Such as Continue in His Word?

JOHN 8, 30—32.

As He spake these words, many believed on Him. Then said
Jesus to the Jews which believed on Him, If ye continue in My
Word, then are ye My disciples indeed; and ye shall know the
truth, and the truth shall make you free.

"All Scripture is given by inspiration of God." The
Bible is God's Book. God's words, God's thoughts, are
herein laid down for our salvation. Upon this topic I re-
cently preached to you. Now, when God gives us a book,
is it to be marveled at that we find thoughts therein which
far transcend all human reason? Is it to be marveled at
if we find mysteries here which we cannot fathom? Would
it not rather be marvelous if we could grasp all that God
says? God is infinite, we are finite; how impossible for
our small, finite mind to understand the infinite mind
of God! What, then, should be our attitude over against
the Bible? Accept, believe, what God has deigned to
reveal to us just as it reads. And that is the very thing
God demands of us. Again and again we are enjoined:
"Hear the word of the Lord"; "Thus saith the Lord."
We are bidden to "bring into captivity every thought to
the obedience of Christ." That is the attitude of the
Lutheran Church over against the Bible, the Word of God.
And for that very reason, because we bow in humility to
the Word, we are reviled as a sect that is everywhere
spoken against.

"Toleration" is the watchword of our time. "Do not
condemn this or that doctrine of the other Protestant
Churches simply because they differ from yours," we are
told. "You have your view, they have theirs; who can
tell which is correct? Instead of fighting one another, let

us rather unite and sweep the world for Christ." Honeyed words, indeed, that appeal to human reason, but treacherous words, nevertheless, because they give God the lie. God speaks in this Book, and we should say: "Speak, Lord; Thy servant heareth." "How can this be, how that?" such questions should find no room in our hearts. God speaks. What does He say? "What readest thou?" This is the all-important question; the *how* we leave to God. Such is the attitude of the true disciple of Christ. This to-day's text teaches. Let us, therefore, consider:

What Does Christ Say of Such as Continue in His Word?

1. They are His disciples indeed.
2. They shall know the truth.
3. The truth shall make them free.

1.

In the section from which our text is taken Christ had discoursed on Himself as being the Light of the world. The words made a deep impression on many of His opponents; they wrought faith in their hearts. *"Then said Jesus to those Jews which believed on Him: If ye continue in My Word, then are ye My disciples indeed."* What Jesus here says holds good for all times.

His true disciples are such, He says, as continue in His Word. That is plain speech. Now, *what is Christ's Word?* Self-evidently, not only the few words that He here spoke to the Jews, but all the words that are recorded of Him in the Bible. Is that all? No, Christ is God; the whole Bible is given by inspiration of God. The whole Bible is God's Word, Christ's Word. As we read the New Testament, we find that the writers everywhere speak of the Word of God and that of Christ as interchangeable terms, as being one and the same thing. God's Word is Christ's Word.

And now, who is a *disciple* of Christ? "Disciple" one was called who believed in Christ, an adherent, a follower, of Christ. In that final commission of His, He said to His eleven disciples: "Go ye, therefore, and make disciples of all nations, baptizing them in the name of the Father and of the Son and of the Holy Ghost; teaching them to observe all things whatsoever I have commanded you. And, lo, I am with you alway, even unto the end of the world." Here we plainly see who is a disciple of Christ. It is one who is baptized into the name of the Triune God, one who through faith is intimately connected with Him — a believer. A disciple of Christ is one who is taught to observe not this or that or the other thing, but all things which He has commanded. Christ is the Master, He commands; the disciple, the believer, is to observe what He commands.

And not only were the believers called Christ's disciples while He sojourned visibly with them on earth, but after His ascension they were still His disciples. And wherever the apostles went to carry out His commission and established churches, the believers were called His disciples — in Jerusalem, in Ephesus, in Antioch, and in other places. How was that possible? In His high-priestly prayer to the Father He had said of His disciples: "I have given them Thy Word." John 17, 14. And He had assured His disciples: "He that heareth you heareth Me, and He that despiseth you despiseth Me; and he that despiseth Me despiseth Him that sent Me." Luke 10, 16. Now, whosoever believed the word of the apostles, which was the Word of Christ, became Christ's disciple. The Gospel the apostles and their associates preached was the "Gospel of Christ." 1 Cor. 9, 12. Aye, Paul in express words calls it the Word of Christ when he exhorts the Colossians: "Let the Word of Christ dwell in you richly in all wisdom." And through this Word we, too, have become believers, disciples, of Christ.

And who are Christ's *true* disciples? He Himself says: Those who *"continue in His Word,"* i. e., adhere to His every word, accept it just as it reads. A believer is a disciple, a learner; Christ is the Master. A disciple, being a learner, does not criticize his Master, does not doubt His word or set it aside. If he does that, he no longer is a disciple, but a master in his own mind, who virtually says: Though the master says so and so, yet I shall not accept it because I cannot understand what He says. A true disciple says: One is my Master, Christ! In His Word I will continue.

And now, who is this Master, Christ? "God over all," "the mighty God"; and you infinitesimally small creature would have the audacity to criticize, to set aside, His Word? Is that the attitude of a true disciple? No, says Christ, a true disciple adheres to My every word; thus I would have My disciples act. Thank God, my friends, we belong to the Lutheran Church, whose attitude is to bow to every word of Christ, of the great God, and hence Christ says also of us: "Ye are My disciples indeed."

· 2.

Not only does Christ laud such as adhere to His Word, His true disciples, but He gives them the glorious assurance: *"Ye shall know the truth."* What a glorious thing in this age of doubt, of unrest, of skepticism, to know we possess the truth, the absolute truth! Are we certain of possessing the truth? Yes. How do we know? Christ says so. What does He say? When have we the truth, God's truth? *"If ye continue in My Word."* That is plain. Take My Word, read it, understand it just as it reads, and adhere to it, then you shall know — what?

The truth. He does not say: "If you do not understand this or that, try to harmonize My Word, try to make it acceptable to human reason." He does not say: "Ask, How can this be? and if you do not understand the *how*, reject it." Christ says of Himself: "I am the Truth." He cannot err. Now, if we continue in His Word, we have the truth, we cannot err. Are all opposing doctrines wrong? Yes. Why? There is but one truth.

"What arrogance of the Lutheran Church!" we hear some one say. "Other preachers are more liberal; they say, 'This is my view of this doctrine,' or, 'Jesus here seems to say,' or, 'In my opinion the apostle would say.'" But, friend, is that teaching God's truth? Is it not rather teaching doubts? Is that according to the apostle's exhortation to contend for the faith once delivered to the saints? Is that honoring Christ? No. He says: Continue in My Word, and ye shall know the truth. This is the one infallible rule to arrive at the truth according to the promise of God. What is not truth is a lie. Sad to say, such a simple, self-evident statement finds little favor in our times of wishy-washy theology. Said a noted English divine a few years ago: "People look at you with amazement if you suggest that there is such a thing as fixed truth, and they eye you with supreme contempt if you dare to assert that the opposite of truth must be a lie. You must be some old fogy or antediluvian, or you would never make such an observation. The sooner you are back in Noah's ark, the better. . . . A man says that black is white, and I say that it is not so. But this is not kind to say it is not so; you should say, Perhaps you are right, dear brother, though I hardly think so. . . . If they hear a sermon that cuts at the root of sin and deals honestly with error, they say, 'That man is very narrow-minded.'" — Well, we will bear the accusation. Was Paul narrow-minded? What does he say to the Galatians, who were in danger of being led astray by perverters of the Gospel of Christ? "But though we or an angel from heaven preach any other gospel unto you than that which we have preached unto you, let him be accursed." Gal. 1, 8.

My friends, "pure doctrine" is not a phrase to be sneered at. A heathen Pilate may scoffingly ask, "What is truth?" implying that truth is not to be found; but a Christian prays: "Sanctify us in Thy truth; Thy Word is truth." He abides by the word of His Master: "If ye continue in My Word, ye shall know the truth." Let us apply the test. God says: "All Scripture is given by inspiration of God"; "Holy men spake as they were moved by the Holy Ghost." Thereby we abide; hence the Scriptures are the Word of God. God tells us that the world was created in six days of twenty-four hours each; thereby we abide, and we know the truth. Scripture says of Baptism: "Baptism now saves us." How can water do such great things? reason asks. God says so, and thereby we abide; hence we know the truth. Christ says: "This is My body; this is My blood." Matthew, Mark, and Luke so testify; the Apostle Paul corroborates it; hence, in the Lord's Supper we receive, under the bread and wine, the Lord's true body and blood. How is that possible? We do not know. Christ says so, and by His words we abide; hence we know the truth. Brethren, we condemn the false *doctrines* of the other Churches, not the *people*. Thank God, He has His children there also; but these His children are not begotten by the errors taught there unwittingly perhaps, but by the truth which in some measure is still preached among them. People are born again, not of corruptible seed, but of incorruptible, by the Word of God, which liveth and abideth forever. 1 Pet. 1, 23. Let us thank God that without any merit or worthiness in us He has given us the truth as it is in Christ Jesus.

But if we continue in the Word of Christ, we not only are His true disciples and know the truth, but *"the truth shall make us free."*

3.

Our text speaks of making people "free." Freedom — oh! that is a word to conjure with in our days. . Freedom, political freedom, social freedom! An age of freedom for the oppressed and downtrodden! Such are the catchy phrases that fall from the lips of multitudes of speakers and are found in a vast number of modern books. Will this much- heralded freedom ever be attained? Never! It is but a favorite phantom, pursued by such as know nothing about the true freedom in Christ. Christ says: *"The truth shall make you free."* Not the much-lauded toleration, not boastful science, not state laws, but the truth, *i. e.,* the Gospel of Jesus Christ. This, and this only, has the power to confer true freedom. What does Christ mean when He says: "The truth shall make you free"? The explanation follows in the text. "If the Son shall make you free, ye shall be free indeed." It is the freedom the Son of God has merited by His sufferings and death, and which those possess who believe in Him; it is the freedom from the dominion of sin, from the accusations of the devil, the freedom from eternal death and its terrors and from the tortures of hell. This heavenly, spiritual freedom only he attains who possesses the truth.

To illustrate. If sin would accuse us, we answer: "It is God that justifieth." If the Law would terrify us, we reply: "Christ is the end of the Law for righteousness to every one that believeth." If cares of this life assail us, the apostle consoles us: "Cast all your cares upon Him, for He careth for you." If death rises before us in all its awfulness, the Word of Truth assures us: "Death, where is thy sting? Grave, where is thy victory? But thanks be to God, which giveth us the victory through our Lord Jesus Christ." Such is the great spiritual freedom of which Christ speaks.

And where this freedom obtains, the shackles of spiritual slavery are broken. We are free children of God; free to do what Christ has bidden us; free to omit what God does not demand. "One is your Master, even Christ; and all ye are brethren." In the Church of Rome there is slavery, spiritual slavery. Antichrist sits in the temple of God and gives commandments as a god. The priests durst not marry, meat must not be eaten on such and such days, this must be done and that other thing — all man-made precepts of which the Word of God knows nothing, and of which it says: "In vain they do worship Me, teaching for doctrines the commandments of men." And round about us in various other denominations we, too, perceive the straining at gnats and the swallowing of camels. Perverting the words of Paul, they say: "Taste not, touch not, handle not," this, that, and the other thing.

No, we are bidden to continue in Christ's Word; to that we are bound, upon that we must insist as His true disciples, and then we shall also walk as His disciples in holiness over against God and righteousness toward our fellow-men. Knowing the truth, we can boldly confront all gainsayers with a "Thus saith the Lord," that sure and safe weapon of truth. Knowing the truth, we are free children of God, who are saved by faith in Christ Jesus. And when death comes, we know that through Christ we are free from the power of the devil, sin, and death, and that we shall enter into the eternal freedom above, where Christ has gone to make a place for us. Amen.

The Creation of the World.

HEB. 11, 3.

Through faith we understand that the worlds were framed by the word of God, so that things which are seen were not made of things which do appear.

Whence is this world upon which we mortals dwell? Did it produce itself, or was it created by a Supreme Being, by an all-powerful and all-wise Creator? We Christians know that the latter is the case. Our authority for this belief is unimpeachable too. Scripture says: "In the beginning God created the heaven and the earth." Throughout the Old and New Testaments this truth is reiterated. But right here we are told with a condescending smile: That old Bible-record of the creation of all things which tells us that the earth was created in six days six thousand years ago was good enough when civilization lay in its swaddling-clothes, but to-day, in the light of scientific research, it must be discarded as a myth. Science has taught us the doctrine of the evolution of all matter.

Well, what is evolution? There are various schools. Says one would-be authority *: The "vast multitudes of plants and animals existing to-day have resulted from simpler forms, and these from still simpler, and these again from simpler still, down and down to some ancient simplest types. This needs no argument for the cultured reader of the present day." Even at the risk of being considered uncultured by this writer, however, we shall have the temerity to ask a few questions: Where did these first simple types come from? What is the mechanism of this evolution? Science says, "I don't know." Well, how do you know what you think you know? It is a hypothesis, we are told. What is that? "A scientific guess." Well,

---

* *Harper's Monthly*, January, 1909.

but a scientific guess is a contradiction in itself; science means to know by observation or experience; hence, there is no such thing as "a scientific guess"; either you know or you guess. If I know that I have ten dollars in my pocket, I do not have to guess at the fact; if I do not know, I may guess; but that is not "a scientific guess."

We question the writer a little further: Is this the only "scientific guess" that has been made about the creation of the world? "No," he answers; "years ago there was a *Nebular Hypothesis* by Laplace, but it is no longer tenable; it should be discarded." But was not that believed as an established fact by the people at that time? "Yes, people forgot that it was a hypothesis, a guess, and accepted it as truth." And now people are to believe the "scientific guesses" of to-day as established facts? How unreasonable! A generation from to-day new guesses will be made, and your cult will keep on making bad guesses and never arrive at the truth.

Where did *matter* come from? Science says, "I don't know." For to say: A particle of matter happened to exist from which all else developed, will satisfy no thinking mind. Where did this *particle* come from? Again, granting the particle, where did *living* matter come from? One scientist says: "The source and origin of living matter was borne to the earth from another planet." Immediately we ask, Where did this *planet* come from? Science says, "I don't know." But another scientist raises his voice in protest: "No," says he, "living matter began on the *earth*." When we ask where and in what form it began, science says, "I don't know." And when we urge the question, How can *life* come out of *dead matter?* science says, "I don't know." The writer of the article in question says: "The heavy air above and the water below on the land possessed the essential elements of living matter. Ages and ages passed, and these lifeless elements appeared as "living beings." We interpose: You assume too much. Where did the air and the water and the land you speak of come from? You do not know. Granting the air and the water, how could they combine to create life? How can life come out of dead things? Science answers, "I don't know." "The *how* of their uniting is the eternal enigma," says this scientist, and he concedes it to be incredible that *lifeless* sea-water and air, acting through blind chemical laws, can evolve *living matter;* hence he concludes that there was a "guiding Intelligence" at work. What this "guiding Intelligence" was the writer cannot say. — Other scientists speak of a cell that God imbued with life. Out of this cell, in millions and millions of years, the earth, and all there is thereon, evolved.

"There is nothing more unreasonable than the creed of the unbeliever, notwithstanding all his prattle about the excellence of reason." (Bettex.) Just one instance to show how foolish some of the assumptions of the unbelievers are. The ape, we are told, finally developed into man. How? Ages ago the ape walked on four legs. In order to obtain his food, he was compelled to climb trees and reach for food with his forelegs. He became an expert in the use of these legs, and by constant stretching they finally assumed the shape of our arms and hands. In choosing his food, it was necessary for him to exercise his judgment. By constantly using his forelegs in reaching for his food and by constantly exercising his judgment, this faculty gradually attained to greater perfection, until the wonderful brain of man was fully developed, and the nerve system connecting forelegs and head also developed more and more, until, through the use of his forelegs, the ape had also physically become the noblest of all creatures, called man. Verily, "professing themselves to be wise, they became fools." And still, thousands of people profess to believe this worse than nonsense. Their minds are so constructed as to believe any perplexing phenomenon satisfactorily explained when some eminent philosopher gives it a name.

Again, if we question these learned men about the age of the earth, they agree to disagree. In 1862 one scientific guesser (Lord Kelvin) assumed its age to be between twenty and four hundred million years. The same authority, a few years later, modified his statement to from twenty to forty million years. Another guess by another guesser (Ioly, 1899) put it at eighty to ninety million years. The latest estimate credits the age of the earth to be "not above seventy million nor below fifty-five million." In other words, scientists do not know. "Scientists" they call themselves, that is, "men who know," but the fact is they are "scientific guessers," or simply — guessers.

Evolution does not explain anything. To say ages ago there was a tiny particle from which all else evolved is simply evading the question. The question remains, Where did this particle come from? The tinier the particle, the greater the miracle. To say God created a cell in which there was life, and from this all else sprang, is calling for greater faith than the Bible demands. For this cell-theory involves thousands of miracles where the Bible demands but one. Even from the standpoint of human reason it is true what one eminent thinker of our day (Bryan) says: "Go back as far as we may, we cannot escape the creative act, and it is just as easy for me to believe that God created man as he is as to believe that millions of years ago He created a germ of life and endowed it with power to develop into all that we see to-day."

I have dwelt so long on this topic to show you how little science knows about the creation of the world, and how unreasonable science is. Sad to say, these evolutionistic ideas have crept into text-books used in the public schools. Still sadder, even some preachers, instead of planting themselves squarely on the impregnable Scriptures, have accepted the theistic evolution idea in order to appear to be up to date. They ought to know that the whole thing is born of unbelief, that it has been handed down by the ancient heathen, and that it is diametrically opposed to the Scriptures.

Finally, with us Christians the question is not, Which is easier to believe? but, What says the Lord? "Heaven and earth shall pass away," says He that cannot lie, "but My words shall not pass away." Now, what does the Bible say about

The Creation of the World?

In agreement with our text we shall speak

> *1. Of the fact of creation;*
> *2. Of the manner of creation.*

1.

"Through faith we understand that the worlds were framed by the word of God, so that things which are seen were not made of things which do appear." "Things which are seen," says the text, *i. e., "the world,"* all that exists in time, have not their being from *"things which do appear,"* from things which are manifest to our senses. That emphatically impresses the fact upon us that there was no material at hand out of which the "things seen" could have been made; there were no earthly germs, substances, or cells preexistent from which the finished product of creation as we have it to-day could have evolved. The creation of the world was the act of producing things out of nothing. This statement, so simple, yet so sublime on account of its very simplicity, brands all the evolutionistic theories regarding the creation of the world, advanced by so-called scientists, as falsehoods and lies.

Our text is in full harmony with the very first sentence

of the Bible: "In the beginning God created the heaven and the earth," so much so, indeed, that an explanation of it is at the same time an explanation and elucidation of our text. "In the beginning God created the heaven and the earth." Incontrovertibly, then, God already existed in the beginning, aye, before the beginning of things. Besides Him there was nothing that had existence. "Before the mountains were brought forth, or ever Thou hadst formed the earth and the world, even from everlasting to everlasting, Thou art God," says the psalmist.

"In the beginning God created the heaven and the earth." The phrase "in the beginning" precludes the notion of the eternity of matter. This world of ours had a beginning. "Of old hast Thou laid the foundation of the earth; and the heavens are the work of Thy hands." In the light of these majestic dicta of Scripture, how absurd, nonsensical, and puerile are the vague mouthings of the evolutionists!

"In the beginning God created *the heaven and the earth.*" That was the actual beginning of the world's history, the beginning of all things, the beginning of time. Heaven and earth were *created.* They did not arise by a process of emanation, nor were they evolved from any preexistent primeval material. The statement simply reads: "God *created* the heaven and the earth *in the beginning,*" which means: When as yet there was no material existence, God brought this world into being by His almighty creative power. *"Things which are seen were not made of things which do appear."* "He spake, and it was done; He commanded, and it stood fast."

From the foregoing explanation the meaning of the word "create" becomes patent. Prior to the beginning of which our text speaks only God was in existence, nothing else besides Him. God called into being this universe. How? Out of nothing. Hence, to create means to make out of nothing. The making of heaven and earth is a creation out of nothing. By His creative word, "Let there be," God, the Triune God, called into existence the things that were not. Rom. 4, 17. *"Things which are seen were not made of things which do appear."* This truth is corroborated by various passages of the New Testament. Four thousand years after the creation of heaven and earth, St. Paul, versed in the philosophical systems of the heathen, writes to the Colossians: "By Him [Christ] were all things created that are in heaven and that are in earth, visible and invisible." "All things," whether animate or inanimate, rational or irrational, "all things" that have existence, were produced by His creative power. Observe that the apostle speaks of "things," complete things, that were created. There is no room here for a slow process of evolution. This comprehensive term "all things" the apostle specifies by saying: that are in heaven and that are in earth." Wheresoever things may exist, in heaven or in earth, they have all been created by Him. St. Paul furthermore says: "all things, visible and invisible"; that is to say, of whatever nature the things may be, they are His handiwork. He created the visible things, such as the earth with its flora and fauna; the luminaries of the heaven, the sun, the moon, and the myriads of stars, and last, but not least, man, the crown of creation. He called into being the invisible things, by which Paul, according to the context, primarily understands the heavenly world of spirits, the thrones, dominions, principalities, and powers. In short, as the last book of the New Testament declares: "God created heaven, and the things that therein are, and the earth, and the things that therein are, and the sea, and the things that therein are."

How vain are the imaginings of those self-styled scientists who endeavor to substitute a vapory theory of evolution for the doctrine of creation! How flatly Scripture denies

atheism, polytheism, pantheism, and all other cognate
"isms"!

On the other hand, what great consolation this doctrine
of the creation of heaven and earth by God Almighty
affords us Christians! This God, who has created heaven
and earth, is our dear Father in Christ Jesus. He, the
Almighty, can care for us and help us in every need. With
Him all things are possible. With firm confidence we
may and should trust in His divine guidance, saying with
the psalmist: "I will lift up mine eyes unto the hills from
whence cometh my help. My help cometh from the Lord,
which made heaven and earth." And again: "Our help
is in the name of the Lord, who made heaven and earth."

2.

God created heaven and earth. Having considered this
fact, let us now learn of the *manner* in which God performed this miraculous work. *"The worlds were framed
by the word of God,"* we read in our text. God said, "Let
there be light!" and there was light. Through this
almighty *fiat* of God, things that did not exist before came
into being. "He spake," and it was done. The world
sprang into existence by virtue of the omnipotent word
of God.

The doctrine of the creation of the world is an *article
of faith.* "Through faith we understand that the worlds
were framed by the word of God." Hence we confess in
the Creed: "I believe in God the Father Almighty, Maker
of heaven and earth." But does not Rom. 1, 18—20 say
that natural man can know of the existence of God by
virtue of his reason, that he can know "by the things that
are made" that there is a Creator? Is there a contradiction
between these two passages? By no means. When contemplating nature, the light of reason tells us that of itself,
by accident, this world could not have come into being.

It must have had a rational, supernatural, wise, divine author. Beyond this, however, reason cannot argue. How this universe was made reason cannot fathom. That it was made by the word of God reason cannot know. Reason says: "Nothing can issue from nothing." Matter must have been extant from which the world was made. Therefore the text says: "Through *faith* we understand that the worlds were framed by the word of God." Through what faith do we understand this? Through faith in the Word of God as it is recorded in Gen. 1, Ps. 104, and other passages treating of this article of faith. All those passages are God's Word, therefore true. This we believe, upon this we rely, and consequently we are divinely certain as to *how* this world was created, all the vain babblings of science, falsely so called, to the contrary notwithstanding. Scientists are fallible men; God, who speaks in the Scriptures, is infallible. He, the Creator, knows more about His handiwork than all the geologists and germ theorists put together. Where the statements of scientists and those of the Bible clash, the Bible must prevail, for it is the absolute truth from Genesis to Revelation.

And this Book of Truth, moreover, says plainly: "In six days the Lord made heaven and earth." And these days are natural days as our days are, consisting of a period of light and a period of darkness succeeding one another. Read the record of Creation in Genesis, and you will find that the days are marked by "evening" and "morning." It reads: "And the evening and the morning were the first day"; "And the evening and the morning were the second day," and so on to the sixth day. It is absolutely impossible for an unbiased Christian reader to find anything else than six natural days described here. Again, at a much later period in the history of God's people, when God established the Sabbath as a day of rest, He said to Israel: "Six days shalt thou labor and do all thy work."

Why labor six days? "For in six days the Lord made heaven, and earth, and the sea, and all that in them is." The scientists say: The days in the record of Creation do not mean natural days, but periods of time extending over millions of years. But here God speaks of those very six days of Creation. How plain the words are: "Six days shalt thou labor and do all thy work . . .; for in six days the Lord made heaven, and earth, and the sea, and all that in them is"! If the scientists were right, this would mean: "Six days," each day extending over millions of years, "shalt thou labor and do all thy work. For in six days," each extending over millions of years, "the Lord made heaven and earth." You perceive what nonsense the scientists would have us believe.

But, says one, does not the Bible say that "one day is with the Lord as a thousand years and a thousand years as one day"? True — "with the Lord"; but when Moses says: "The evening and the morning were the first day," "the second day," etc., he does not speak of God's days, eternity, in which there is no succession, no beginning, no end, but of days of creation, each of which had a beginning and an end.

But how is all this possible? Because God is God. His name is Omnipotence. He might have created heaven and earth in six minutes or in six hours, but it pleased Him to do it in six days. How do we know? Scripture says so. How is it possible? How can these things be? We answer with the psalmist: "Our God is in the heavens"; that is the seat of His sovereign majesty and power and glory. He is not a man-made, impotent idol (see the context), but the almighty God; "He hath done whatsoever He hath pleased." Amen.

Divine Providence.

(For Bible-passages quoted in this address, see Catechism, Qu. 120 ff.)

In the First Article of the Creed we confess: "I believe that God has made me and all creatures; that He has given me my body and soul, eyes, ears, and all my members, my reason and all my senses." God is the Creator. We furthermore believe that He preserves and governs me and all creatures.

Of God's Preservation and Government of the World

we would speak to-day. The subject is vast. We shall not attempt to go into details. Basing our discourse on various passages quoted in the Catechism under this doctrine, we shall endeavor to give it in bold outline.

In Acts 17, 27. 28 we read: *"God is not far from every one of us; for in Him we live and move and have our being."*

Athens, the center of culture, art, literature, and science, knew not God. She proclaimed her ignorance loudly to all the world on one of her temples by the humiliating inscription: "To the Unknown God." Paul saw the city wholly given to idolatry, and his spirit was stirred within him. On the summit of the Areopagus, Christianity and paganism met. Confronted by adherents of the Stoic and the Epicurean systems of philosophy, pantheists and atheists, surrounded by temples filled and ornamented with gods and goddesses, the objects of heathen idolatry, Paul discourses on the *creation,* the *preservation,* and the *government* of the world by this "Unknown God."

From this masterful oration the passage just quoted is taken. Having told the Athenians "that God made the world and all things therein," Paul goes on to say: "It is He that giveth unto all, life and breath and all things."

God created the world; it still exists. God created us; we exist. The existence of the world, our own existence, is not due to self-preservation, but to God's sustaining power. He gives to all, life, that is, life in itself; not only that, but He gives to all, breath, the continuation of life by means of breathing; not only that, but He gives to all, all things, everything necessary to maintain this life.

The true God, Paul furthermore says, is in no way similar to your dead idols enthroned in the Temple of Mars near by or in the Parthenon below me. In the temples made with hands the Deity does not dwell. *"He,"* God, *"is not far from every one of us."* The true God is nigh us; He protects us, sustains us. *"In Him we live"* — without Him we should have no life. *"In Him we move"*— without Him we could not move from place to place, we could not lift our arms or open our mouths. *"In Him we have our being"* — without Him we should have no existence at all.

This was strange doctrine to the heathen philosophers of that day; it is a matter of jest to the philosophers of our day. Worldly-wise philosophers, "men of science," as they like to style themselves, whether of the first century or of the twentieth, are but ignorant idolaters.

Though God could preserve our lives without any earthly means, and though He could provide the necessaries of life directly, still it is His good pleasure to provide for our sustenance *mediately.* In the sweat of our brow we are to earn our livelihood. Who does not want to work shall not eat, says the apostle. But it is God who preserves our strength, our skill, etc., which enables us to obtain our daily bread. It is He that promised: *"While the earth remaineth, seed-time and harvest, and cold and heat, and summer and winter, and day and night, shall not cease."* It is He that *"maketh His sun to rise on the evil and on the good and sendeth rain on the just and on the unjust."*

It is He that "giveth rain in his season; He reserveth unto us the appointed weeks of the harvest." Our meat, *i. e.,* our food, our nourishment, is a gift of God. *"Thou givest them their meat in due season."* And for Him it is a trifling matter to provide for the millions of His creatures. He has but to *"open His hand,"* and they are satisfied. May God through His Word lead us to know this more and more, so that we may receive our daily bread with thanksgiving! Then, while performing the work of our calling industriously, we shall commit the success of our labor to God and thus escape the carking cares for the morrow.

It is God that preserves man; it is He that preserves the *world.* We read in Hebrews: *"He upholds all things by the word of His power."* If God would withdraw His hand from this world but for a single moment, it must collapse, chaos must ensue. "God has not forsaken His work, as the architect leaves the house when it is finished, but He preserves all things and governs them by His paternal providence." Of God's government of the world the psalmist says: *"The Lord looketh from heaven; He beholdeth all the sons of men. From the place of His habitation He looketh upon all the inhabitants of the earth. He fashioneth their hearts alike; He considereth all their works."*

God is not unconcerned about the affairs on earth. "He looketh from heaven," and of all the millions of people not one escapes His all-seeing eye; for "He beholdeth all the sons of men, He looketh upon all the inhabitants of the earth." Nor is He an idle spectator, allowing men to do as they please, but "He fashioneth their hearts alike," *i. e.,* He fashions the hearts of them all, "He considereth all their works." All things and all the affairs of men are in His hands, subject to His control and direction. *God's government extends even to the smallest and most trifling matters.* This comforting truth is beautifully set forth in the Lord's words: "Are not two sparrows sold for a farthing? And one of them shall not fall on the ground without your Father. But the very hairs of your head are all numbered." The word "farthing" was used among the Greeks to designate any small, insignificant amount. Its value, in our money, is about five-eighths of a cent. "And yet" God cares for the sparrows; one of them shall not fall on the ground — dead — without God's permission. To the sparrows God stands but in the relation of the Creator to the creature. To you, however, He stands in the relation of a father to a child. Emphatically God is called "your Father." The Creator, who cares for the meanest of His creatures, *e. g.,* the sparrows, will He not care for you, His child, whom He has bought with a price? Why, you are so precious in His sight that His care extends to the very hairs of your head, trifling matter as that may seem. Every one of them is numbered.

As to sinister designs that evil men may plan against God's children, we know that He can easily *overrule them for good.* The words Joseph spoke to his brothers are in point here: *"Ye thought evil against me, but God meant it unto good, to bring to pass as it is this day, to save much people alive."*

Joseph had been sold into slavery by his brothers. They *"thought evil against him."* Reason asks, Why did God not prevent this abominable deed? God, looking into the future, "meant it unto good." Not only did Joseph become a great man, — thus evil turned into good for him, — but God, controlling the evil, brought it to pass that thus much people were saved alive. Among those saved alive were the very brothers of Joseph. It was also for their welfare that God overruled their evil act. They did not deserve it, but God is kind.

In brief: *Troubles and afflictions may assail the Chris-*

tians, the cross will cross their threshold, yet there shall not be a real evil in this, for it comes from the loving hand of God and is not sent for their hurt, but for their good, as St. Paul expressly declares: *"We know that all things work together for good to them that love God."* "Now, no chastening for the present seemeth to be joyous, but grievous; nevertheless, afterward it yieldeth the peaceable fruit of righteousness unto them that are exercised thereby." "They that sow in tears shall reap in joy. He that goeth forth and weepeth, bearing precious seed, shall doubtless come again with rejoicing, bringing his sheaves with him."

Trials of faith produce cares. But these cares are not to make us doubt God's grace and mercy. We Christians know: Our heavenly Father cares for us. Hence we are exhorted: *"Commit thy way unto the Lord, trust also in Him, and He shall bring it to pass."* The entire course of our life is here pictured as a way over which we Christians travel to reach our heavenly destination. On this way there are obstructions to impede our progress — trials, cares, afflictions manifold, are encountered. What are we to do in the face of such dangers? *"Commit thy way unto the Lord,"* or as St. Peter says, *"Cast all your care upon Him,"* and then, whatever may betide, trust in Him, as in a most faithful Counselor and Guide and an ever-present Help in every need, and *"He shall bring it to pass,"* He will bring it to a good issue. Appropriating the words of the psalmist, we may confidently exclaim: "Yea, though I walk through the valley of the shadow of death, I will fear no evil; for Thou art with me; Thy rod and Thy staff, they comfort me."

All divine blessings spoken of in the preceding passages the Lord showers upon "them that fear Him," upon the Christians. *What impels Him to do it?* Any merit or worthiness in us? No; God owes us nothing. *"When ye shall have done all those things commanded you, say, We are unprofitable servants: we have done that which was our duty to do."* So, even though we had fulfilled all the commandments of God, the idea of merit would be excluded. Moreover, though we belong to the number of those who fear Him, yet we are sinners and do not deserve to be helped. David's plea must ever remain ours: "Enter not into judgment with Thy servant." What, then, prompts God to bless us so abundantly? The answer is found in this text: *"The Lord pitieth them that fear Him,"* or as the psalmist says in another place: *"For He is good; because His mercy endureth forever."* God pities us *"as a father pitieth his children."* A fatherly pity, a fatherly mercy, is one such as a dear father entertains and manifests towards his dear children. And since it is the Lord who has pity on us, this mercy is a divine mercy, such as only God can entertain and show, one that is altogether perfect, and one "that endureth forever."

Now, since God does all this purely out of fatherly, divine goodness and mercy, we are constrained to confess with Jacob: *"I am not worthy of the least of all the mercies and of all the truth which Thou hast showed unto Thy servant."*

This is the sentiment of every true Christian. Hence he asks with the psalmist: "What shall I render unto the Lord for all His benefits toward me?" And the answer is found in Ps. 118, 1: "O give thanks unto the Lord; for He is good; because His mercy endureth forever." Amen.

Sin in the Light of the Word of God.

1 JOHN 3, 4: Sin is the transgression of the Law.

1 JOHN 3, 8: He that committeth sin is of the devil; for the devil sinneth from the beginning.

ROM. 5, 12: By one man sin entered into the world and death by sin.

IS. 64, 6: We are all as an unclean thing, and all our righteousnesses are as filthy rags.

EPH. 2, 3: And were by nature the children of wrath.

ROM. 7, 7: By the Law is the knowledge of sin.

ROM. 10, 4: Christ is the end of the Law for righteousness to every one that believeth.

It is an awful subject of which I want to speak to-night, one that, alas! is made light of and ridiculed by the majority of mankind. My subject is *Sin*. The doctrine is so vast that I can present it merely in outline.

What is the essence, the nature, the character of sin? "Sin," says St. John, "is the transgression of the Law." 1 John 3, 4. So sin is not what you or I think ought to be called sin. Your idea or mine as to what should constitute sin counts for nothing. God is our Creator; we are His creatures. God, the Ruler of the universe, has given a Law in which He very definitely says what is right and what is wrong in His sight. His Law is embodied in the Ten Commandments. And the sum and substance of this Law is: "Thou shalt love the Lord, thy God, with all thy heart and with all thy soul and with all thy mind," Matt. 22, 37; "Thou shalt love thy neighbor as thyself," Matt. 22, 39; and: "All things whatsoever ye would that men should do to you, do ye even so to them," Matt. 7, 12.

This is God's Law. Now, sin is the transgression of this Law. Why? Because God has said so. The State of Illinois has laws; this city has laws by which it is governed. Some of them, you may think, are unjust; but transgress any one of them, great or small, and you have violated the law and are punishable. What you think about these laws makes no difference. Just so with the Law of God. Any transgression, any departure from this rule of God, His Law, is sin. Whether that transgression be small or great has nothing to say — in every case you have offended the majesty of God, the Lawgiver. And you may sin, and do sin, against this Law by omission as well as by commission, by neglecting to do what God demands, as well as by acting contrary to His will. By way of illustration: You may lose your property by neglecting to pay your taxes, as you would if you squandered your possessions by riotous living. Says Scripture: "To him that knoweth to do good and doeth it not, to him it is sin." Jas. 4, 17. Measured by this rule of the divine Law, the world is full of sin. How godless, therefore, the teaching of the Christian Scientists, who say there is no sin! Beware of this delusion of Satan!

What is the origin of sin? "The devil sinneth from the beginning," 1 John 3, 8; that is to say, the devil made the beginning of sin, he was the first to sin, he was the originator of sin. Created holy and righteous, the devil "kept not his first estate, but left his own habitation." And how did sin enter into the world? "By one man," says Paul, "sin entered into the world." This "one man," Adam, voluntarily permitted himself to be blinded by the devil's deceit and craftiness. Turn to Genesis 2; there you have the sad story of the Fall. God had said: "Of the tree of the knowledge of good and evil, thou shalt not eat of it; for in the day that thou eatest thereof thou shalt surely die." There was a command, a law, of God. In Genesis 3 we read that at the instigation of Satan our first parents "did eat." There was the transgression. Thus "sin entered into the world"; for St. Paul says, speaking of this very same transgression of Adam: "Wherefore, as by one man sin entered into the world and death by sin, and so death passed upon

all men, for that all have sinned." This guilt of Adam
was imputed to his descendants. Adam had lost the con-
created image of God; he now was a sinner. And hence
we read: "Adam begat a son in his own likeness"; mark
well, not in the image of God, but in his own sinful likeness. Thus Adam dragged all mankind into sin. And
now every person by nature, because he is a sinner, is in
the power of the devil. For "he that committeth sin is
of the devil," is minded like the devil.

This sin inherited from Adam we call *original sin.*
It consists in the utter absence of the image of God.
"In me," says Paul, "that is, in my flesh, dwelleth no good
thing." We are constantly inclined towards all that is
evil. "The imagination of man's heart is evil from his
youth." Our entire human nature is wholly depraved,
and the powers of the intellect and will are perverted, while
those of the body are impaired. So great is this depravity
that "by nature we are dead in sins"; so enormous, that
on account of this original sin alone we are subject to
damnation. "We were by nature the children of wrath,
even as others." This doctrine of original sin may be
pooh-poohed by some, but that does not do away with the
awful reality. People so inclined would do well to study
their Bibles more carefully. The babe in the cradle is
not innocent in the sight of God, but as it is by nature, it
is an object of His wrath. That remains true because the
words of St. Paul read: "We were by nature the children
of wrath." Speaking of little children's being innocent
does not even show keen observation of child-nature. Every
mother knows how easily the old nature of the child asserts
itself. — Again, that phrase about the "fatherhood of God
of all men" is a terrible delusion. No man has a right
to say, "Abba, Father," who is not a Christian; for before
he has been born again, he is under the wrath of God, and
his father is the devil.

This original sin is inborn, is inherent, and is *transmitted from parents to children.* David says: "Behold, I was shapen in iniquity, and in sin did my mother conceive me." And Christ says to Nicodemus: "That which is born of the flesh is flesh."

And this original sin is the fountain from which flow actual sins, be they evil desires, thoughts, words, or deeds. "Out of the heart proceed evil thoughts: murders, adulteries, fornications, thefts, false witness, blasphemies."

My friend and fellow-sinner, do you know that you are a sinner? Perhaps you say: "Well, I suppose I must concede that I am a sinner; we are all sinners." No, no; that is not what I mean. Do you know what it is to be a sinner? Do you know that to be a sinner means to be damned? "Well," you say, "I'm not so good as I might be, but I am a good deal better than Mr. So-and-so and Mrs. So-and-so, and they claim to be Christians; so I think my chances for being saved are pretty fair." Let me tell you, you do not know what sin is. You must either turn or burn! You are applying a wrong standard of measurement to yourself. A little boy once found a broken carpenter's rule which was but six inches long. In his ignorance he mistook it for a foot-rule. He measured himself and, running to his mother, said, "I am seven feet high." He had taken his measure, it is true, but his measure was wrong. His height was no more than three and one-half feet.

Now, what is the *rule* wherewith we are to measure ourselves before God? Paul answers: "By the Law is the knowledge of sin." Rom. 3, 20. If, therefore, you would have an adequate knowledge of sin, do not look at your neighbor, but search the Law. It is a mirror which will show you your true image in the sight of God. Its demand in brief is this: "Be ye holy, for I, the Lord, your God, am holy." Be ye as holy as I am, the holy God, who knows no sin. Let all your desires, thoughts, words, and deeds be good and holy; from the day of your birth till the day of your death not an unholy, sinful thought must have arisen in your mind, much less a sinful word have passed over your lips or a sinful deed have been committed by you. The Law says in awful thunders from Mount Sinai: "Thou shalt! Thou shalt not!" And if thou transgressest the will of God, damned thou art! "Cursed be he that confirmeth not all the words of this Law to do them!" Deut. 27, 26. This is God's holy will. God must punish sin. His holiness and His justice demand it. Here are His unalterable words: "Cursed be he that confirmeth not all the words of this Law to do them!"

Perhaps you will say: "I live according to the Golden Rule." Do you know the Golden Rule? "Therefore, all things whatsoever ye would that men should do to you, do ye even so to them; for this is the Law and the prophets." Do you know that this is a summary of the Sermon on the Mount, where Christ, expounding the Law, had said, just to mention a few things: "Thou shalt not kill" and had added, in explanation of this commandment, that "whosoever is angry [in his heart] with his brother" is a murderer in the sight of God and just as damnable as he who commits the actual deed? Furthermore He had taught: Whosoever looketh on a woman to lust after her is an adulterer in the sight of God. The angry thought, the lustful look, are damnable sins before God. Now, you Golden Rule people, how will you escape the vengeance of a wrathful God?

Suppose a painter possessed the art of painting your heart as it is in the sight of God, would you be willing to hang it in your parlor and display it with admiration to your friends? On this picture would be every sinful desire, every lustful thought, every angry word, every evil

deed you have ever been guilty of. Would you be willing
to have it painted? There are sins you have committed
ten, twenty, thirty years ago — you have forgotten them,
and you may think God has forgotten them. No, never.
Why, though you had forgotten them, though they had
been committed in secret, though your wife, your husband, did not know of them — this moment they stand
before your mind's eye and make you shudder. You have
not forgotten them; did God forget them? Thou, God,
"hast set our iniquities before Thee, our secret sins in
the light of Thy countenance."

Do you still imagine in the hardness of your heart:
"Oh, God will overlook this sin and that. Though I did
break one commandment, I have tried to keep the rest"?
Listen! There are *ten* commandments, but there is but
one Law. These ten commandments are but as ten links
in a chain. Suppose you were suspended from a burning
house with a chain having ten links, and your life depended
on that chain. If one link of this chain would break,
down you would go to certain death though all the other
links were still good. Just so with the Law of God, the
Ten Commandments. Break but one in desire, or thought,
or word, or deed, and you have violated the whole Law,
and the curse rests upon you; for, "whosoever shall keep
the whole Law and yet offend in one point, he is guilty
of all." Sinner, if you have no substitute to avert the
wrath of God, you are doomed!

Or is there still a lurking idea in your mind suggesting:
"I have done some good things in my lifetime, and I hope
God will take these as an equivalent for my shortcomings"?
Again a delusion and a snare of the devil! What must
even the Christians confess regarding their good works?
"We are all as an unclean thing, and all our righteous-
nesses," all our good deeds, "are as filthy rags." Mind you,
when Isaiah, the man of God, weighs himself in the scales

of God's justice, he does not say: "All our *sins* are as filthy rags," but, "all our *righteousnesses,*" all our good deeds, "are as filthy rags." "Filthy rags" — did you ever consider what these words say? Rags! You cannot clothe yourself with rags, neither can you cover your guilt by your supposedly good works; in the sight of God they are but rags. Not only that, they are "*filthy* rags." In the large cities you often notice rag-pickers going about looking for rags. Oftentimes they have a stick, with a hook attached to it. In sewers and gutters they hunt for rags. But they do not pick them up with their hands, the rags are too filthy; they hook them, full of dirt and mire as they are, and throw them into their bag. Such filthy rags are your good works in the sight of God. Such is the picture of him who would barter his so-called good works for salvation.

Oh, fellow-sinner, have you seen your true image in the mirror of God's holy Law? Has the picture made you tremble? Have you come to a realization of the awfulness of sin? I hope so. Moses, the man of God, says in Ps. 90, 7. 8: "For we are consumed by Thine anger, and by Thy wrath are we troubled. Thou hast set our iniquities before Thee, our secret sins in the light of Thy countenance." Oh, what an awful day will that last Great Day be for the sinner when he must give account of every idle word! When his whole life, with all evil thoughts, sinful desires, and works, even the secret sins, will be revealed to all mankind; when all these sins will be put "in the light of His countenance," where shall the sinner appear?

Thus the Law reveals our sins, but it cannot save us. The Law is a mirror wherein we behold our sinful image, but the mirror cannot cleanse us. It shows us the disease of sin, but gives no cure; it damns us. It causes us to cry out, "I am lost."

Have you come to a conviction of your sin? Do you

tremblingly ask, "Is there no help?" Look! Look to Calvary! There you see the precious blood of the Lamb of God slain for your sin, the blood flowing from His wounds for you. Look to Christ, "who Himself bare our sins in His own body on the tree." He is your Substitute. He took your place. The vials of God's wrath over sin are emptied upon His innocent head. The Just takes the place of the unjust. Christ became a curse for us. Look! I plead with you, look to the Lamb of God, which taketh away the sins of the World! Where are your sins and mine? On the cross. "The handwriting that was against us" is blotted out. "The blood of Jesus Christ, His Son, cleanseth us from all sin." Sinner, look to Christ! "The Lord hath laid on Him the iniquity of us all." "Christ is the end of the Law for righteousness to every one that believeth." The Savior says: "Him that cometh to Me I will in no wise cast out." Come to Him and be saved. Amen.

Why Need We Not Be Ashamed of the Gospel of Christ?

ROM. 1, 16. 17.

For I am not ashamed of the Gospel of Christ; for it is the power of God unto salvation to every one that believeth; to the Jew first and also to the Greek. For therein is the righteousness of God revealed from faith to faith, as it is written, The just shall live by faith.

"I am ready to preach the Gospel to you that are in Rome also; for I am not ashamed of the Gospel of Christ." These are words from the pen of the great Apostle Paul that ought to fill every true preacher of the Gospel with holy courage. On his three great missionary journeys Paul had but one great theme for a dying world: "Christ and Him crucified." At Antioch, at Thessalonica, at Philippi, at Ephesus — everywhere his central topic was:

"Jesus is the Christ." On these journeys, which extended over thousands of miles, Paul met with Jew and Gentile, with men of high and low degree; but whatever their nationality or their station in life, in one thing they were all alike — they were sinners, and for such there is salvation in but one name: Jesus.

Paul had several times purposed to go to Rome to preach the Gospel there also, but he had been prevented from doing so. So he wrote his Epistle to the Romans. Rome was the mighty metropolis of the world. Here lived "the then modern men with advanced ideas"; here were "people of cultural attainments." What is Paul going to preach to them? He declares: When I arrive at Rome, I shall preach the old Gospel. I am not ashamed of it.

Here is a lesson for us. To-day we hear and read much about "the religion of the modern man." The modern man is supposed to be the man of intellect, of cultural attainments; he lives in an enlightened age. The "dogmas of a less enlightened age" are buried for him. He needs them not. To tell him that "in Christ alone there is salvation" is a shelf-worn dogma; to tell him to get down on his knees and cry out with the publican from a deep conviction of sin: "Lord, be merciful to me, a sinner!" is an insult to his high moral character. In fact, it matters little, we are told, what you believe, whether it be Buddhism, Confucianism, Eddyism, Russellism, or any other "ism," just so you live right and do right — that's the test of being a Christian! I know of a man that so thought and so lived, and so do you — the Pharisee in the Temple.

Preachers who have this conception of the religion of the modern man are not in harmony with St. Paul, they are out of place in the pulpit; they are ashamed of the Gospel of Christ.

What, then, is the religion, the doctrine, that is to be preached to "modern man"? That question has been authoritatively answered once for all times by the Head of the Church. In His last Great Commission He says: "Go ye into all the world and preach the Gospel to every creature. He that believeth and is baptized shall be saved; but he that believeth not shall be damned." "And, lo, I am with you alway, even unto the end of the world."

Here is the will of the Master: Preach the Gospel till the end of the world.

True to the Master's injunction, the disciples preached this Gospel, and the Church grew; and true to his Master's will, the greatest of all apostles, Paul, preached this Gospel everywhere and to everybody, to Jew and Gentile, to the wise and the foolish, and so, as he emphatically assures us, even in imperial Rome he will preach this despised Gospel, since he has good reasons not to be ashamed of it.

As Paul says, so say we. Let us inquire:

Why Need We Not Be Ashamed of the Gospel of Christ?

1. Because of its glorious contents;
2. Because of its divine power.

1.

"I am not ashamed of the Gospel of Christ; for it is the power of God unto salvation to every one that believeth." "Gospel" is a term used by many, but understood by few. Gospel means "glad tidings." So the Gospel contains tidings, news, which are to make men, sinners, glad, joyful. Sinners, however, can be made glad by one news, and one only, and that is the tidings of the forgiveness of sins. And this is exactly what the word Gospel means: glad tidings of the forgiveness of sins. Plainly we see this from the text. It is called "the Gospel *of Christ"*; it is the glad tidings that speak of Christ, the Savior, and what He has done for fallen mankind. What was the only purpose of Christ's coming into the world? Paul tells us: "Christ came into the world to save sinners." So the Gospel tells

us of our salvation, and so the text has it: the Gospel is a power of God *"unto salvation."* "For God so loved the world that He gave His only-begotten Son, that whosoever believeth in Him should not perish, but have everlasting life." Truly, these are glad tidings! Without them not a single soul can be saved. Is there any higher wisdom than the wisdom which teaches us how to attain eternal life? Need we be ashamed of such a Gospel?

Expressed in other words: Why is the Gospel such glad tidings? *For in this Gospel "is the righteousness of God revealed from faith to faith."* What does that mean? Righteousness is the condition of one who is just, who satisfies all the demands of the Law. A person who possesses righteousness is one with whom God Himself can find no fault; he is one of whom God says: I look upon you, and must look upon you, as one who is holy, just, sinless.

Now, where in this wide world is such a man to be found? Let us make inquiries of the best. Here is Paul. What does he say? "I know that in me, that is, in my flesh, dwelleth no good thing." Here is Isaiah. He says: "We are all as an unclean thing, and all our righteousnesses are as filthy rags." David confesses: "Enter not into judgment with Thy servant; for in Thy sight shall no man living be justified." John, the Apostle of Love, declares: "If we say that we have no sin, we deceive ourselves, and the truth is not in us." So the inspired writers who say: "They are all gone aside; there is none that doeth good," "All we like sheep have gone astray," speak the truth.

But in order to be saved, we must be righteous in the sight of God. "Be ye holy, for I am holy." "Cursed is every one that continueth not in all things which are written in the Book of the Law to do them!" These are God's demands.

Where is there a way of escape? None, as far as we

could devise. The wisest of the wise, neither in Paul's time, among "the then modern men with advanced ideas," nor in our own times, among the modern men in their self-conceived wisdom, have discovered a way to turn a sinful soul into a righteous one. And the modern men with all their advanced ideas and their vaunted high moral character and good-fellowship will be damned to the uttermost hell if they have not a righteousness that availeth before God.

Where is this righteousness to be found? Only in this despised Gospel. "For therein is *the righteousness of God revealed from faith to faith.*" And it is not a righteousness obtained by living right and doing right, as the "religion of modern man" teaches, but it is *a righteousness by faith,* and only he who hears this Gospel and believes it is in possession of it.

How this righteousness came about Paul does not say here. This text is but the theme, which he unfolds later on, saying that, since neither Jew nor Gentile could keep the Law, both must be damned, but that God in His mercy had sent His only-begotten Son, who fulfilled the Law's demands for us, and that whosoever believeth in Him should not be eternally lost. "Christ is the end of the Law for righteousness to every one that believeth." This righteousness of Christ imputed to us by faith is the righteousness of God, *i. e.,* the only one that availeth before God; and it is the "righteousness *of God,*" *i. e.,* it is a divine righteousness, because Christ, the true God, has procured it for us. Christ, God, has fulfilled God's commands, and thus he who relies on Christ possesses divine righteousness. This is the glorious message of the Gospel. Need we be ashamed of it?

Note, too, that the apostle says of this righteousness that it was *revealed* to us. "None of the princes of this world," as Paul says in First Corinthians, none of the people of "cultural attainments," none of the men of the "most advanced ideas," could have thought out such a glorious plan of salvation. God's wisdom was necessary thereto.

And now, who possesses this righteousness? Let us ask Paul. He says: "Who shall lay anything to the charge of God's elect? It is God that justifieth." Ask Job. He answers: "I know that my Redeemer liveth." Ask the thousands of martyrs, the millions of Christians, and with one voice they cry out: "The blood of Jesus Christ, His Son, cleanseth us from all sin."

Take a look into yonder world. Who are those in white robes and with palms in their hands? They are they that have come out of great tribulation and have washed their robes and made them white in the blood of the Lamb; they are they who have appropriated this righteousness by faith — they live, live eternally. "The just shall live by faith." Such are the glorious contents of the Gospel.

2.

The preacher of the Gospel proclaiming to his people in the name of God the glorious message of the Gospel knows not only that he is announcing the highest wisdom of God, but that by that same message he is *imparting* the wonderful things of which the Gospel treats. The apostle says: "I am not ashamed of the Gospel of Christ, *for it is the power of God unto salvation.*" The Gospel, wherever it is preached, is a power of God, a divine power. Through the Gospel, God exerts His divine power; when the Gospel is preached, God is active through that Word, exerting His gracious power upon the hearts of men. This Gospel, though preached by men, is not man's word, but the Word of God; hence its divine power. When the governor sends a message through a messenger, the messenger does not impart any power to the message; it is powerful because it comes from the governor; it is his word; he backs it. So here.

And God's Word *is* powerful. In the beginning He said, "Let there be," and this world sprang into existence. And when this Word, this Gospel, is preached, it is God's powerful Word that works to a certain end. Which? The Gospel is a power of God *"unto salvation."* By and through this Word, this, to natural man, foolish preaching, salvation is imparted. New worlds are not created by it, but even a greater thing is performed by this Gospel. It converts man, kindles faith in his heart, and thus saves him. Behold the power of this Gospel! Are we to be ashamed of it?

But, you say, I do not quite understand the drift of your argument. Very well. How is man by nature? Dead, spiritually dead. "Natural man receiveth not the things of the Spirit of God," that is, the Gospel, "neither can he know them, for they are foolishness unto him." Now, let all the modern men with advanced ideas, with culture, refinement, and what not, come together and awaken this spiritually dead man. Can it be done? Just as little as the armies and navies of the world combined could awaken one dead person in your cemetery.

But what is impossible to man, to angels and archangels, God's Word does, does to-day, and will do to the end of days.

By the Law, God casts down the self-righteous Pharisee, shows him his sinfulness and damnableness, and pronounces the curse upon him. And when man in the anguish of his soul cries out, "Woe is me! I am lost, lost forever, because I have sinned against a righteous God!" and the Gospel is preached to him, he sees Jesus as his Savior and through it receives power to accept Him, and the Gospel formerly despised by him as foolishness is now heavenly wisdom unto him. Thus this Gospel is a power of God unto salvation. And in the power of this Word the formerly spiritually dead person is now spiritually alive; he walks in the newness of life, has power to overcome sin, yea, power to face death.

As many redeemed as are standing before the throne of God, as many millions as to-day are translated from the kingdom of Satan into Christ's Kingdom of Grace, so many million witnesses there are for this saving power of the Gospel. And they testify, having experienced the power of the Word, that it is a power of God unto salvation, not to every one that worketh, that "does right and lives right," but *"to every one that believeth."* Faith in Christ Jesus is the only thing that saves, because it grasps that righteousness which avails before God. Is there any reason to be ashamed of this powerful Word?

But let us illustrate this power of the Word. On one of his missionary journeys Paul came to Philippi. There he spoke the Word of Truth to some women. Among them was Lydia, a seller of purple. And we are told that, when Lydia heard Paul speak the Word, "the Lord opened her heart that she attended unto the things which were spoken of Paul" — and she believed. Here is a practical commentary to our text: "The Gospel is the power of God unto salvation."

Again, in Philippi, Paul and Silas were thrown into prison. At midnight suddenly there was a great earthquake, the foundations of the prison were shaken, the doors stood ajar, and the prisoners' bands were loosed. The jailer, ready to commit suicide, was restrained from doing so by Paul. In the anguish of his heart the jailer asks, "Sirs, what must I do to be saved?" Paul answers: "Believe on the Lord Jesus Christ, and thou shalt be saved." Paul and Silas, we are told, "spake unto him the Word of the Lord and to all that were in the house. And the jailer rejoiced, believing in God with his whole house."

To him and his house the Gospel had become a power of God unto salvation.

In the godless city of Thessalonica, Paul and Silas preached the Word for three Sabbath-days, and, behold, a church was gathered of such of whom Paul later writes: "Ye turned to God from idols to serve the living and true God." Such is the power of the Gospel. It is a Word of Life that imparts life. Truly, the Gospel is a message we Christians need not be ashamed of.

One point that we wish to impress upon you this evening is this: Nowhere outside the Lutheran Church do you hear this doctrine of the Word's being such a powerful means to bring one to salvation. In other denominations you may hear the exhortation again and again, "Come to Jesus!" but how to come to Jesus they know not and say not.

But, Lutheran friends, since we know of the glorious contents of this Gospel and its divine inherent power, we are under a serious obligation. Which? Can the seed that is not planted in the field manifest its power? No. Neither can the Word if it is not planted in our hearts. Hence we must let this Word dwell richly among us, so that it can manifest its power more and more.

Why is it that within congregations where the Word is taught in its purity so little of its power is oftentimes manifest? Is it the fault of the Word? No. "The Word of God is quick and powerful." The fault lies with us; we do not use the Word as diligently as we should.

Hence, let us hear the Word diligently, gladly learn it, read it at home individually and at family worship. The more we do this, the more shall we learn of its glorious contents and the more and better experience its divine power; we shall experience that it is a power unto salvation, a Gospel of peace, a Gospel of truth, a Gospel of eternal life. Amen.

The Deplorable Condition of Natural Man in Spiritual Things.

1 Cor. 2, 14.

The natural man receiveth not the things of the Spirit of God, for they are foolishness unto him; neither can he know them, because they are spiritually discerned.

On Mount Olivet, two miles east of Jerusalem, Jesus held His last converse with His disciples. He spoke to them of things pertaining to the kingdom of God and promised them the outpouring of the Holy Spirit. "And while they beheld, He was taken up, and a cloud received Him out of their sight." Acts 1, 9. True to His word, ten days after His ascension, the Spirit came. That day was a day of gladness for the disciples, and the Church still celebrates with rejoicing the day of Pentecost as one of her great festivals. The history of that event is well known.

Now, we must not think of the coming of the Holy Spirit merely as a thing of the past. The Holy Spirit still comes, not in a miraculous, extraordinary manner, as on that first day of Pentecost, but still He comes, not amidst the groaning and shrieking of audiences, whose nerves are unstrung by hair-raising harangues or by sensational preaching, — but He comes. He comes in the means of grace, for our salvation.

"How am I to understand this?" some one may ask. "Salvation has been prepared by Christ for all men. That was His mission in the days of His flesh. He ascended into heaven and now sits at the right hand of the Father. The victory is won; our enemies are conquered. What, then, is there still to be done by the Holy Spirit?" True, the work of redemption is finished, but if we are to enjoy the blessings of Christ's redemption, the salvation He procured must become our own. How is this done? You answer, "By faith in Christ Jesus." But can man by nature believe in Jesus Christ? No. "I cannot by my own reason or strength believe in Jesus Christ or come to Him." This coming to Jesus in true faith is the work of the Holy Ghost. Without the Holy Spirit's work we would remain in darkness and in the shadow of death; without the Holy Spirit's work no one could be saved; without the work of the Holy Spirit there would be no Church, no communion of saints, no true piety, nothing but a world full of paganism. Hence the Holy Spirit's work is indispensably necessary for our salvation.

In order to see this more clearly, let us consider, under the guidance of the Holy Spirit: —

The Deplorable Condition of Natural Man in Spiritual Things.

1. *Man by nature has not, and cannot have, any knowledge of the Gospel.*
2. *Man by nature is hostile to the Gospel.*

1.

Throughout the chapter from which our text has been chosen, the apostle contrasts the spiritual and the natural man. The spiritual man has saving knowledge. The natural man has not. There is, furthermore, a contrast between the wisdom of God, manifested in the Gospel, and the wisdom of man. In the course of the development of this thought the apostle says: *"The natural man receiveth not the things of the Spirit of God; for they are foolishness unto him; neither can he know them."* Whom the apostle means by "natural man" is well known. It is man as he is by nature, apart from the grace of God, not yet illumined by the Holy Spirit. The expression *"the things of the Spirit of God,"* wrenched out of its context, may seem difficult to understand at first sight, but viewed in the connection in which it stands, it becomes very simple. The apostle says: "We speak not the wisdom of this world, but the wisdom of God," "the hidden wisdom which God ordained before the world unto our glory," *i. e.,* the plan of salvation through Jesus Christ. How did we learn of these things? "God hath revealed them to us by His Spirit; for the Spirit searcheth all things, yea, the deep things of God. . . . Now, we have received the Spirit which is of God that we might know the things that are freely given to us of God." Which things? The Gospel of Jesus Christ. "We speak in the words which the Holy Ghost teacheth. *But the natural man receiveth not the things of the Spirit of God."* Now, plainly, what are "the things of the Spirit"? The Gospel of Jesus Christ.

Our text says: "The natural man receiveth not the things of the Spirit of God," the Gospel. *"Natural man receiveth not,"* cannot apprehend, cannot understand, the Gospel. The apostle speaks of natural man's intellect, for not to "receive," to understand, to know, to discern, to judge of spiritual matters, points to the inability of the intellect. Natural man's intellect is blind in spiritual matters. However keen his intellect may be in matters mundane, however great things he may accomplish in the various sciences, things marvelous to behold, still of the Gospel, though it may be preached to him ever so plainly, he understands nothing. This is what the apostle says: "The natural man receiveth not the things of the Spirit of God." He does not say, "Natural man's intellect is weak in spiritual matters"; he says "it receives nothing," it is blind. And he predicates this of natural man in general. The most learned has no advantage over the most illiterate.

The second statement is even stronger: *"Neither can he know them."* Natural man has absolutely no capacity

for spiritual things. It is impossible for him to understand them. Given the best teacher, the most approved
method, and yet Darwin's most highly developed ape cannot
grasp the mathematical problem of Euclid. The ape may
put on a wise face while following the demonstration, but
he is a brute and has no capacity for mathematics; he
cannot understand it. So with natural man in spiritual
matters — he has no capacity for them. Why this utter
inability? *"For they are spiritually discerned."* The
things are spiritual, and he is unspiritual. A blind man
knows nothing of colors; a deaf man knows nothing of
music; an unspiritual man knows nothing of spiritual
things. With emphasis it is said: "Neither *can* he know
them." Natural man is not like another Hercules at the
parting of the ways; he is not a free agent here, so that
he could either accept or reject the Gospel. He can do but
one thing: reject it. Natural man's condition is deplorable,
indeed. The same apostle who writes these things to the
Corinthians reminds the Ephesians of the fact that they
were "dead in trespasses and sins." "Dead" — that word
adequately describes natural man's condition. "Dead" —
there is no spiritual life in natural man, not a spark of it.
What was the consequence of this spiritual death? They
walked "in trespasses and sins." Such was natural man
then, such he is now.

How is this dead man to come to life? By his own
powers? Absurd question! He is dead; he has no power.
Is there not at least something good in natural man that
is pleasing to God? Why, he is dead — "dead in trespasses
and sins"! How are the blind eyes of natural man to be
opened? How is this dead man to be brought to life?
By virtue of his own powers, through his own exertion?
Why, he is dead! You might more reasonably expect the
dead in your cemetery to awaken themselves to physical
life and to walk the streets of your town than to see a spir-

itually dead man awaken himself to spiritual life. How, then, is he to be brought to spiritual life? Through the work of the Holy Ghost.

Does some one perhaps say: "The preacher is over-stating the lamentable condition of natural man"? Why, friends, we are simply unfolding the thought of the apostle and saying what every true Christian who contemplates his former condition knows to be true. No, natural man's condition is even more deplorable than we have stated so far; for not only is he blind in spiritual matters, not only is he dead to spiritual life, but *he is even hostile to the Gospel.*

2.

"The natural man receiveth not the things of the Spirit of God; for they are foolishness unto him." When the Gospel is preached to natural man, he not only does not receive it, and not only does he not understand it, but he is so perverted that he does not even recognize the fact that these things are too deep for him, and that he should therefore modestly say: I do not understand them; they may be true, but I cannot see them so. No, he acts as though he were perfectly competent to sit in judgment on these matters. What is his judgment? *"Foolishness!"* When a philosopher discourses on the system of his philosophy, let us say, to a body of wise doctors of medicine, the doctors, as rational men, will say: "Mr. Philosopher, your talk was very interesting, but beyond our grasp. What you say may be true, and we shall not contradict you, but we cannot understand it. We are medical men." The next day the philosopher takes sick, and he goes to the doctor. "I understand philosophy," he says, "but not medicine. What ails me? Prescribe some medicine for me." Each is wise enough to keep in his own sphere. Again: You hold up a color-plate to a blind man and say, "Describe the colors." He replies, "Absurd demand! I cannot;

I am blind." But *here* is a blind man — natural man —
who has not even sense enough to know that he is blind
in spiritual matters. Here is a man — natural man —
who has absolutely no capacity for, no knowledge of, divine
things, and yet he dares sit in judgment on divine matters.
The Gospel of Christ is preached to him, and he says, "It is
foolishness!" He is told, "Christ is both God and man,"
and he says, "Foolishness!" He is told, "This God-man
would be your Savior," and he says, "Foolishness!" He is
told, "Believe in Jesus Christ and be saved," and he says,
"Foolishness!" He is told, "Accept the Gospel and be
eternally happy." "Accept the Gospel?" he sneers; "accept
foolishness? No, I reject it, I spurn it, I ridicule it; away
with it!" Friends, such is the attitude of natural man
towards the only hope of his salvation. The wisdom of God
he adjudges foolishness. Salvation is purchased, God is
reconciled, but he spurns both. On he goes to the precipice.
Another step, and down he goes into the awful abyss, crying, as he falls to destruction, "Foolishness! Foolishness!"
How did this come about, this awful condition of natural
man? Through the Fall of our first parents.

Nor is this all. His hostility manifests itself still more.
The apostle says in another place: *"The carnal mind is
enmity against God."* Natural man, who in one respect
is dead to spiritual life, in another sense is very much
alive, *viz.,* in his hatred against God. He is angry with
God for having given the Ten Commandments; he hates
God for having given the Gospel; he hates God when he
hears that he is to be saved by a foreign righteousness.
He wants to be his own Savior; he believes he will be able
to answer God on Judgment Day! He lives in opposition
and rebellion against God. "The carnal mind is enmity
against God." Rom. 8, 7. Such is the condition of natural
man painted in faint colors.

So, then, here is the state of affairs briefly. On the

one hand, salvation is acquired by Christ: "God was in Christ, reconciling the world unto Himself." On the other hand, man is dead in trespasses and sins, without even the desire to be saved. How can life be instilled into this spiritual corpse? Only and alone through the work of the Holy Spirit, and He does it through means, the means of grace, the Gospel. Through the Word that is preached the Holy Ghost is active; through it He operates on man's heart with divine power. Through the Word He imparts sight to the blind, life to the dead; through it He takes away the enmity against God, so that "he that came to scoff remains to pray."

See the necessity of the work of the Holy Ghost! Hence we confess: "I believe that I cannot by my own reason or strength believe in Jesus Christ, my Lord, or come to Him; but the Holy Ghost has called me by the Gospel." Briefly this work is described by St. Paul thus: "No man can say that Jesus is the Lord but by the Holy Ghost." Whoever can truthfully say: Jesus of Nazareth, true man, is at the same time Lord, "God over all," confesses the mystery of mysteries: "God is manifest in the flesh"; he also believes that Jesus is his Lord. And whoever believes that Jesus is his Lord, says the apostle, has received such power only through the Holy Ghost.

In conclusion: Have *you* received the Holy Ghost? Do you know that you are a sinner? That is the work of the Holy Ghost. Do you believe in Jesus Christ as your Savior? That is the work of the Holy Ghost. Do you pray in your closet? That is the work of the Holy Ghost. Do you love to hear the Word of God? That is the work of the Holy Ghost. Do you battle against sin? That is the work of the Holy Ghost. . Do you find consolation under the cross in the Word? That is the work of the Holy Ghost. Do you comfort yourself with the promises of eternal life? That is the work of the Holy Ghost. Happy are you, for

you are the temple of God, and the Holy Ghost dwells in
you. May He abide with you, with me! Let us pray: —

> O Holy Ghost, descend, we pray;
> Abide with us from day to day,
> Thy temple deign to make us.
> Let Thy bright beams, Thou heavenly
> Light,
> Dispel the darkness of the night,
> To joy and gladness wake us.

Do this for Christ's sake. Amen.

Justification by Faith Alone.

ROM. 3, 28.

Therefore we conclude that a man is justified by faith, without the deeds of the Law.

Page after page might be filled with praise of Luther
and his work from the pens of acknowledged authorities
outside the Lutheran Church. Summarized briefly, this
is what they say: No Luther, no religious and civil liberty,
no liberty of press and speech, no separation of Church
and State, no Declaration of Independence, no Constitution
of the United States in its present form, but a priest-
ridden country such as our next-door neighbor, poor Mexico,
is to-day. All true, very true. But great as are these
material blessings, they are simply but by-products of the
Reformation and do not touch its real significance at all.

Wherein, then, does the real greatness of Luther consist? *Luther was God's chosen vessel to restore the glorious
Gospel of the free grace of God by faith in Jesus Christ.*
This doctrine, *justification by faith,* as it is commonly
called, the very heart of the Gospel, had been buried for
centuries under papal rule. Before the Reformation
spiritual darkness covered the earth. In the temple of

God sat Antichrist as though he were God, but the voice of Jehovah was not heard there. When an anxious sinner asked, "What must I do to be saved?" he was not told, "Believe on the Lord Jesus Christ, and thou shalt be saved," "The blood of Jesus Christ, God's Son, cleanseth us from all sin," but the answer was this: Do the works the Catholic Church has prescribed, pray to the saints for their intercession at‑the throne of God, pray especially to Mother Mary; but if you would be fully assured of God's favor, merit it by entering a cloister or a convent. Not a word about the Savior from all sin! Luther relates that in the days before God had opened the Gospel to him, he became pale and terror-stricken at the very mention of Jesus' name, for he had been taught to think of Him as of an angry judge, not as of a loving Savior. "If this is not darkness," he declares, "I know not what darkness is."

How had this dense spiritual darkness come about? In only one way was it possible: Forbidden by the Pope to be read, *the Bible with its glad tidings of Jesus had become an unknown book.* But when the truth of that wonderful Pauline passage, "The just shall live by faith," flashed upon Luther's mind, then it was that he saw the absurdity of the whole papal system of meritorious works, then it was that the cardinal principle of Scripture had been rediscovered. And when that agent of the Pope, Tetzel, toured the country, selling forgiveness of sins, past, present, and future, Luther nailed his Ninety-five Theses to the door of the Castle Church at Wittenberg in defense of the Bible-doctrine — *justification, i. e., remission of sin, by faith alone.* Thus the work of the Reformation was begun October 31, 1517.

Luther's work was a reformation, not a creation. Startling as was this doctrine in his time, still it contained nothing else than the old, old story of Jesus and His love. Salvation by faith in the divine Redeemer, *justification by faith in Christ, that act of God by which He declares righteous all who believe in Jesus, is the Alpha and Omega of the Bible.* By grace alone the sinner is saved. Why, this is the only purpose for which God gave His inspired Book.

Speaking of the Old Testament, Paul says, Acts 10, 43: "To Him [Jesus] give *all the prophets* witness that through His name, whosoever *believeth in Him,* shall receive remission of sins." Christ Himself, speaking of the Old Testament, declares: "Search the Scriptures, for in them ye think ye have eternal life; and they are they *which testify of Me.*" Paul, writing to Timothy, affirms: "The Holy Scriptures" of the Old Testament "are able to make thee wise unto salvation *through faith which is in Christ Jesus.*" 2 Tim. 3, 15. Justification by faith in Christ Jesus — not through works — is the *central* doctrine of the Old Testament. All the prophets of the Old Testament proclaim with one voice: Salvation alone by faith in the Messiah. All the saints in the Old Testament lived and died in this selfsame faith to which Job gives beautiful expression in the words, "I know that my Redeemer liveth."

And as to the New Testament, why, there is not a single page on which is not written: Justification by faith alone! To Nicodemus the Savior says: "God so loved the world that He gave His only-begotten Son, that *whosoever believeth in Him* should not perish, but have everlasting life." Again He says: "Verily, verily, I say unto you: *he that believeth on Me* hath everlasting life." Paul writes to the Ephesians: "By grace are ye saved, *through faith,* and that not of yourselves, it is the gift of God; not of works, lest any man should boast." Again, in our text: "We conclude that a man is *justified by faith,* without the deeds of the Law." But why multiply passages? With one accord the apostles cry out to the perishing multitudes as Paul did to the jailer: *"Believe* on the Lord Jesus Christ, and thou shalt be saved." Aye, indeed, justification, for-giveness of sins, by faith in Christ Jesus is the *fundamental* doctrine of Christianity.

This doctrine, preached by Luther in all its beauty and purity as no other had done since the time of the apostles, soon dispelled the spiritual darkness in which the Pope had enveloped the world. And this doctrine it is, and no other, that to-day deals the death-blow to Papacy in the hearts of the people. This Rome knows. Hence, horrible to say, she *curses* this doctrine of Christ, the prophets, and the apostles, declaring: "If any one says that the ungodly are justified by faith alone, so that it be understood that nothing else is required, let him be accursed." (Council of Trent.) But small wonder Rome does this. For since salvation is by faith alone, pilgrimages to the shrines of so-called saints are useless, prayers to the saints an abomination, purgatory a figment of the imagination, the mass a blasphemy, the priest's claim as a mediator between God and man a lie; and the very Pope, the self-styled vicar of Christ, is deposed. And as for the curse of the Pope, it can harm us none; it is but the curse of Antichrist. To *him* rather apply the words of St. Paul, hurled against the perverters of this very doctrine of justification: "But though we or an angel from heaven preach any other Gospel unto you than that which we have preached unto you, *let him be accursed.*" Gal. 1, 8.

Justification by faith alone — *this is the very doctrine that mankind stands so sorely in need of to-day.* Is it not true that the world is. full of all manner of "isms" and counterfeit religions? Is it not true that from so many pulpits the deity of Christ and His atoning death are denied? Is it not true that so-called Christian ministers publicly declare: "The dogmas of a less enlightened age must be buried for the modern man; live right and do right; character is Christianity"? Why, that is downright heathenism. Poor, deluded people! "They are *without Christ,* strangers from the covenants of promise, having *no hope,* and without God in the world." Eph. 2, 12. *No hope without Christ!*

Over against this rationalistic tendency of the age the Lutheran Church takes a firm and uncompromising stand, crying out aloud: Back to the old paths! Back to the old Bible! Back to the only Savior! She proclaims to a sin-stricken world: "There is no difference, for *all have sinned."* All men, modern as well as ancient, are sinners. "Sin *separates* between you and God." Is. 59, 2. And God pronounces a *curse* upon every sinner: "Cursed is every one that continueth not in *all* things which are written in the book of the Law to *do* them!" Gal. 3, 10. To be a sinner means to be a damned person. "The soul that sinneth, it shall die." All "right living and being good" cannot alter an iota of this solemn truth. Acknowledge this fact; confess with David: "If Thou, Lord, shouldest mark iniquities, O Lord, who shall stand?" Woe me; I am a lost and condemned creature! This is one thing the world must be told; *the damning Law of God must be preached to them.* And if the sinner anxiously inquires: Is there no way of escape from hell? the Gospel must be proclaimed to him; he must be told: Sinner, rejoice *"there is redemption in Christ Jesus."* God, prompted solely by His grace, "sent forth His Son, made of a woman, made under the Law, that He might *redeem* them that were under the Law." This Christ, true man and true God, "was wounded for *our* transgressions, *He* was bruised for *our* iniquities; the chastisement of *our* peace was upon *Him,* and with *His* stripes *we* are healed." Is. 53.

Sinner, here is your Sin-bearer! What must you do to be saved? *"Believe* on the Lord Jesus Christ." Just as you are, come to Him. Through the preaching of the Gospel, God offers to you full and free pardon; He asks nothing of you but to accept this Savior in faith; aye, God Himself will, by the operation of the Holy Ghost, through the Gospel, work such saving faith in you. Rom. 1, 16. Him that believes in Jesus, God justifies, declares righteous, as was done to the publican in the Temple. And this faith in the crucified and risen Savior is a *living, active* faith, productive of works pleasing to God; it is "faith that worketh by love." However, this faith does not justify because of the good works it produces, but because it apprehends the merits of Christ. (*Augsb. Conf.*, Art. 6.)

This is the doctrine the world stands in need of to-day as it did in Luther's time. This doctrine is the *only key* to the whole Bible, and without it the poor conscience can have no true, invariable, fixed hope. This is the doctrine that depletes hell and peoples heaven.

And thou, O Lutheran Church, stand firmly and immovably upon the foundation rock upon which thou hast been built — Christ. Hold aloft to a world perishing in sin thy glorious banner with the soul-saving inscription: "Therefore we conclude that a man is justified by faith, without the deeds of the Law."

Who Is "the Word that was Made Flesh"?

JOHN 1, 14.

And the Word was made flesh and dwelt among us; and we beheld His glory, the glory as of the Only-begotten of the Father, full of grace and truth.

Christmas, the anniversary of the world's greatest event, is the gladdest festival of all the year. The faces of the young are full of glee; the older people forget their age and seem young again; even the sick and decrepit forget their infirmities amidst so much happiness.

There is a reason for all this. Which? More than nineteen hundred years ago a child was born in the village of Bethlehem; a helpless child it was, just like the children of to-day. This child was wrapped in swaddling-clothes and laid in a manger. Mary, its mother, is with the child, and Joseph, its foster-father. And the birth of this child is the cause and source of all this gladness to-day in the hearts of Christians, nineteen hundred years after it has come to pass.

Strange, is it not? No. The story is not all told. From heaven comes a message saying that this child is no ordinary child. Though born so lowly, the entire heavenly host does homage to it. Not far from Bethlehem the angelic choir, all the heavenly host, proclaims to the lowly shepherds tending their flocks this glorious news: "Behold, I bring you good tidings of great joy, which shall be to all people. For unto you is born this day, in the city of David, a Savior, which is Christ the Lord." This is the reason for all this joy we behold to-day — a Savior is born! This child is the Savior! This child is Christ the Lord, the Jehovah, the mighty God! Why, that is the miracle of all miracles — this child the very God! Mary's son, God's Son! Oh, an impenetrable mystery! Verily, Paul's saying to Timothy is true: "Great is the mystery of godliness: God was manifest in the flesh." Our text states it thus: "The Word was made flesh."

Though it is an inscrutable mystery, the fact remains. Unbelievers may scoff and laugh, but that does not overthrow the fact. And what if we cannot understand it? Are there not a thousand things in the universe we do not understand? God be praised, we need not understand it. Joseph and Mary did not understand it. The shepherds who heard the angel's song did not understand it. The Wise Men who came from the East to adore the Christ-child did not understand it. Peter, the great apostle, did not understand it. Paul, the greatest of them all, did not understand it; aye, the very angels in heaven do not understand it: the mystery is too deep even for them; they "desire to look into it." 1 Pet. 1, 12. But though the *how* of the incarnation of the Son of God remains a mystery, Christian faith, kindled by God Himself, grasps the revealed *fact:* "The Word was made flesh . . . full of grace and truth," and thanks Him for His unspeakable gift. Though we cannot fathom the mystery of the incarnation, we may learn a great deal about it. We ask: —

Who Is "the Word that was Made Flesh"?

1. He is true man;   *2. He is true God;*
3. He is our Savior.

1.

"The Word was made flesh." What does this mean? St. John begins his gospel thus: "In the beginning was the Word, and the Word was with God, and the Word was God." Who is this Word? St. John answers: He is "the only-begotten Son, which is in the bosom of the Father." The Son is the Word. So let us substitute the term Son for the term Word, and the meaning will become plainer to our mind: "In the beginning was the Son. And the Son," the second person of the Trinity, "was made flesh." St. Paul expresses the same mystery thus: "Without controversy great is the mystery of godliness: God was manifest in the flesh." God became man. This is the fulfilment of the prophecy of Isaiah, seven hundred years before the event took place: "Unto us a Child is born, unto us a Son is given." And the Evangelist St. Luke, showing the fulfilment of the prophecy, says: "And Mary brought forth her first-born Son and wrapped Him in swaddling-clothes and laid Him in a manger, because there was no room for them in the inn."

Our text proceeds to tell us of this Word that was made flesh, saying that He "dwelt among us." This brief statement describes His visible presence on earth for thirty-three years. On the eighth day after His birth, like all Jewish male children, He was circumcised, and His name was called Jesus. At Nazareth He grew up as "the carpenter's son." Later on He became a teacher of the people, teaching, preaching, and healing in Galilee; He was true man. At Jacob's Well He sat down, being weary of the day's journey. He asked the woman of Samaria to give Him water to drink; He was true man. In the ship on the Sea of Galilee, exhausted from his labors, He fell asleep; He was true man. But why multiply instances? His true humanity was acknowledged by His friends as well as by His enemies. And Scripture expressly calls Him man: "There is one Mediator between God and man, the *man* Christ Jesus." Jesus Himself calls Himself man, "the Son of Man." He said to the doubting disciples: "Behold My hands and My feet that it is I Myself." Hence the writer to the Hebrews says: "Forasmuch, then, as the children are partakers of flesh and blood, He also Himself likewise took part of the same." Christ is true man, the same as we are. Only in one respect was He different from the rest of mankind: "He knew no sin." "He was holy, harmless, undefiled, separate from sinners." "He did no sin, neither was guile found in His mouth." So, who is this Word that was made flesh, this Babe in the manger? It is Jesus Christ, true man, yet without sin.

2.

"The Word was made flesh," says still more, however. It says: The Word, the Son of God, became man, but still remained what He was before — true God. We read: *"And we beheld His glory, the glory as of the Only-begotten of the Father."* So, though He had become man, He still was and is the Only-begotten of the Father, of the same essence with the Father—true God. The angel proclaimed the Babe in the manger to be Christ the Lord, *i. e.,* Jehovah, the great God; and St. John, corroborating this statement, says: There is no doubt about it; "we beheld His glory," we are witnesses thereof; His was a glory exactly like that of the Father. He is in no whit inferior to the Father. His glory and that of the Father are perfectly alike.

And now, what is this glory St. John and his contemporaries beheld? At Cana, Christ turned water into wine. That was a miracle, an act of omnipotence. "And they beheld His glory," says the evangelist. So this act of omnipotence was a manifestation of His glory. He who is omnipotent is God. Christ, then, is God. This glory St. John beheld with wonder and amazement. Christ stilled the tempest-tossed Sea of Galilee — "and they beheld His glory." He healed the leper — "and they beheld His glory." At Nain He raised the widow's son — "and they beheld His glory." He called Lazarus to life — "and they beheld His glory." The disciples saw that this man Christ is more than mere man; they knew that He was also true God.

Do we need further proofs of His deity? No. What Scripture says time and again of this Jesus of Nazareth, that He is true God, is a faithful saying and worthy of all acceptation. God Himself says: "This is My beloved Son, in whom I am well pleased." Christ, too, asserts the same thing. When the disciples of John asked, "Art Thou He that should come, or should we wait for another?" He pointed to His miracles and His preaching, saying, in effect: Judge for yourselves whether or not I am the prophesied Messiah. To the woman of Samaria, who said, "I know that Messias shall come," He replied, "I that speak unto thee am He." Isaiah of old predicts with prophetic vision: "Unto us a Child is born, unto us a Son is given; and the government shall be upon His shoulder; and His name shall be called Wonderful, Counselor, the Mighty God, the Everlasting Father, the Prince of Peace." And Paul, writing to the Romans, corroborates this prophecy by saying: "He is over all, God blessed forever." And St. John says: "This Jesus Christ is the true God and eternal Life." To the Colossians Paul writes: "In Him dwelleth the fulness of the Godhead bodily."

Thus it is true beyond the shadow of a doubt that the Word made flesh, the Babe in the manger, is Christ the Lord, true man and true God, one person with two distinct natures. "Without controversy great is the mystery of godliness: God was manifest in the flesh." "The Word was made flesh."

3.

But now the question arises, *Why* was the Word made flesh? The text answers: "The Word was made flesh and dwelt among us; and we beheld His glory, the glory as of the Only-begotten of the Father, *full of grace and truth.*" That was the purpose of His incarnation: to procure grace. Grace presupposes guilt, and guilt demands punishment. We are sinners by birth. The sentence of the great Judge in heaven reads: "The soul that sinneth, it shall die." Could God revoke this sentence? No. His justice demanded the punishment of the sinner. Satisfaction must be made to the divine Law; grace must be purchased. For this purpose Christ came into the world. He lived, He suffered, He died for us to procure grace. Do you now get a glimpse into the mystery why He became man? Man had transgressed the Law, by man it must be fulfilled. We could not fulfil it; Christ, the man, did; but as no mere man could satisfy infinite Justice, Christ had to be God. And Christ, who is God, is "full of grace," God's grace; this He brought to this earth.

What is the purpose of this grace? It is the "grace that bringeth salvation." Christ came to save that which was lost. So there is no grace of God without Christ. Christ is "full of grace"; but if you are not Christ's, there is no grace for you. There is salvation in none other. He Himself says: "If ye believe not that I am He, ye shall die in your sins." The cure for sin and its terrible consequences is at hand; but if you do not use it, you will perish. The Physician for the sick is at hand; but if He is rejected, death must result.

Do you know that you are a sinner, and that you need grace, God's favor? Then here is your Physician. If you desire to be saved, the Christ-child spreads His arms lovingly to embrace you. And it is immaterial who you are, or what your past life may have been. Emphatically the text says: Christ is "full of grace." His store of grace is inexhaustible, as John says: "We have received grace for grace." The honest, but self-righteous Nicodemus came to Jesus in the night, and he learned that Jesus was "full of grace." Mary Magdalene, the deeply fallen, weeping over her sins, learned that Jesus was "full of grace." Peter would have perished if Jesus, His Savior, had not been "full of grace." Judas need not have perished; for Jesus, His Savior, was "full of grace." And Paul, the "chief of sinners," lived because Jesus, His Savior, was "full of grace." Going up and down in Galilee, again and again Jesus said to each penitent sinner: "Son, daughter, be of good cheer, thy sins are forgiven thee." None that ever came to Him was rejected. He was "full of grace" and is so to-day.

Oh, says one, would that I had lived at that time, that I might have gone to Him with my sin-laden conscience! Do not let this thought trouble you. Though He has withdrawn His visible presence from us, He nevertheless dwells among us even to-day "full of grace." He has established the ministry of reconciliation. He is with us in His Word. His promise is: "He that heareth you heareth Me." You now hear of His grace, His saving grace. This is meant for you. The Savior is born "to all people," as the angel said. "God so loved the world" — this includes you. What are you to do? What did Mary do? and Joseph? What did the Wise Men do who came from the East to seek the Child? One and all, they simply accepted the message in faith. Do likewise. Simply accept, believe, and thank God for His unspeakable gift. Then you will understand the song of the heavenly host: "Glory to God in the highest, and on earth peace, good will toward men." Amen.

Christ Our King.

MATT. 28, 18: All power is given unto Me in heaven and in earth.

JOHN 18, 37: Pilate, therefore, said unto Him, Art Thou a King, then? Jesus answered, Thou sayest that I am a King. To this end was I born, and for this cause came I into the world, that I should bear witness unto the truth. Every one that is of the truth heareth My voice.

2 TIM. 4, 18: The Lord shall deliver me from every evil work and will preserve me unto His heavenly kingdom: to whom be glory forever and ever! Amen.

> All hail the power of Jesus' name!
> Let angels prostrate fall;
> Bring forth the royal diadem
> And crown Him Lord of all!

This beautiful hymn extols Christ, our Savior-King. Of Him and His kingdom we would speak to-day. The subject is so vast that at least three sermons would be required to do justice to it somewhat; but for several reasons we have thought it best to give a comprehensive, though brief, outline of the entire doctrine in one discourse to-day.

Christ's kingship was foretold in the Old Testament.

"Thou hast put all things under His feet: all sheep and oxen, yea, and the beasts of the field, the fowl of the air, and the fish of the sea, and whatsoever passeth through the paths of the seas." And what Daniel saw in the night vision he thus describes: "Behold, one like the *Son of Man* came with the clouds and came to the Ancient of Days; and they brought Him near before Him. And there was given Him dominion and glory and a *kingdom,* that all people, nations, and languages should serve Him." Christ is a king. Hence the inquiry of the Wise Men from the East was: "Where is He that is *born King* of the Jews?"

According to the various subjects and the diverse modes of government Christ's kingdom is threefold: 1. *the Kingdom of Power,* pertaining to all creatures; 2. *the Kingdom of Grace,* pertaining to the Church Militant; and 3. *the Kingdom of Glory,* pertaining to the Church Triumphant. Accordingly we speak

1. Of the Kingdom of Power.

In that final interview with His disciples in Galilee and as a prelude to His last Great Commission, Christ speaks of Himself as the King of the universe. He said: *"All power is given unto Me in heaven and in earth."*

How vast is this kingdom! Christ possesses all power *"in heaven"* — all the holy angels, authorities, powers, the cherubim and the seraphim, are His willing servants. And "in earth," too, "all things are put under His feet." His kingship is world-wide, universal. A grand, a majestic truth! Christ rules and reigns over all, whatever it may be, however powerful it may be, wherever it may be, "in heaven or in earth" — all, all is in His kingdom, the heathen that rage, the kings of the earth and its rulers, aye, the very devils in hell not excepted. His is all power without any limitation. Over all He mightily rules and reigns. This is His Kingdom of *Power!*

And why is it so called? Because the means by which

He rules in this kingdom is, as stated in the text, *"all power." "All power,"* all authority, clearly is *omnipotence.* If His omnipotent word goes forth, who can withstand? And so, "why do the heathen rage, and the people imagine a vain thing? The kings of the earth set themselves, and the rulers take counsel together, against the Lord and against His Anointed, saying, Let us break their bands asunder and cast away their cords from us. He that sitteth in the heavens shall laugh; the Lord shall have them in derision."

Of this "all power," this omnipotence, Christ says, It is "given unto Me." The divine nature of Christ possesses omnipotence as an *essential* attribute, but this essential attribute, by virtue of the personal union, becomes a *communicated* attribute of the human nature. The man Christ is almighty. The God-man was not exalted to royal dignity and power after His resurrection or ascension, but was *born* a King. This "all power," given unto Him according to His humanity, He manifested before His exaltation by numerous miracles, thus proving the truth expressed in our text and in that other saying of His: "All things have been delivered unto Me of My Father." He rebuked the winds and the sea, and they obeyed Him. He walked on the sea. He cast out evil spirits with His word and healed the sick. With a single word He felled His captors. He spoke to him that was dead: "Young man, I say unto thee, Arise; and he . . . sat up and began to speak." The winds, the sea, the evil spirits, the devil, sicknesses, enemies, death — all are subject to His power.

This truth affords great *consolation* for us, since our King so regulates the whole universe and all things upon earth as to contribute to the glory of His divine name and to the gathering and preservation of His Church. And His Church He protects against all enemies, aye, against the very devil himself, for as He, the King, said: "The gates

of hell shall not prevail against it." Why, the very connection in which the words of our text stand to the last
Great Commission of our King prove the same majestic
truth. "All power is given unto Me in heaven and in earth.
Go ye *therefore* and teach [make disciples of] all nations,
baptizing them in the name of the Father and of the Son
and of the Holy Ghost; teaching them to observe all things
whatsoever I have commanded you. And, lo, I am with
you alway, even unto the end of the world." As if to say:
You ambassadors of Mine, be not afraid! You are to wage
war against the formidable kingdom of Satan, to destroy
its bulwarks; and upon its ruins you are to plant the cross,
the emblem of the Crucified One. What a task! But fear
not! "Go ye *therefore,*" since Mine is all power; go
therefore and build My Church. Though you will no
longer enjoy My *visible* presence, *invisibly* I will be with
you, guide you, protect you in the performance of your
sacred office. Disciple the nations, baptizing them, etc.,
and when the last one according to God's decree has been
brought into the Church, then the end will come, and the
scaffold of this world will be torn down, since it has served
its purpose; the *una sancta,* the holy Christian Church,
will be complete. So, then, this "all power," His omnipotence, wherewith our King mightily rules over all creatures, has but one object in view — the gathering and the
preservation of His Church, which is called His Kingdom
of *Grace.*

This universal kingship of Christ is not apparent to
the natural eye. As the writer of Hebrews says: "But now
we see not yet all things put under Him." It is an article
of faith which we are to lay hold of for our consolation.
In yonder life, when the mists will have been lifted from
our eyes and our vision will be clear, when we no longer
know in part, we shall see that this whole universe, together
with its governments, rulers, and ordinances, lay in the

hollow of Christ our King's hands and were made subservient to His gracious purpose — the building of the
Kingdom of Grace. Of this kingdom we shall now speak.

2. The Kingdom of Grace.

In the Gospel of St. John, where we are told of Jesus'
arraignment before Pilate, we read: *"Pilate therefore said
unto Him, Art Thou a king, then? Jesus answered, Thou
sayest that I am a King. To this end was I born, and for
this cause came I into the world, that I should bear witness
unto the truth. Every one that is of the truth heareth
My voice."*

In the trial before Pilate, Jesus had said, "My kingdom
is not of this world," etc., John 18, 36. He spoke of His
special Kingdom of Grace, which, though *in* the world, is
"not *of* this world." Pilate asks, "Art Thou a king, then?"
Jesus, asserting that He, indeed, is a King and describing
the true character of His kingdom, makes answer: I am
a King; I am a *born* King; I am a King of the *truth*.
Who are His subjects? *"Every one that is of the truth
heareth My voice."* Every one "that is of the truth," that
is born of God, whose heart has been conquered and won
by the truth to which He bears witness, belongs to this
kingdom. This is a mark of the true subjects in this
kingdom: they hear *His voice*. Who hears His voice?
The Christians, the believers. And these, collectively,
constitute His kingdom. Wherever the believer may live,
to whatsoever nationality he may belong, whatsoever language he may speak — in the eyes of Christ he belongs
to that "holy nation" of which Peter speaks, 1 Pet. 2, 9.
This kingdom Christ rules by *His voice,* the Gospel, the
Gospel of Grace. Hence it is not a worldly kingdom, but
a *spiritual* kingdom. Speaking to the carnal-minded
Pharisees, Christ says of this kingdom: "The kingdom of
God cometh not with observation" — its coming cannot be

observed by the eyes of the body. "Neither shall they say,
Lo, here! or, Lo, there!" — a definite locality cannot be
assigned to it, — "for, behold, the kingdom of God is
within you," it is of a spiritual nature, has its seat in the
heart. There the King erects His throne and fills it with
joy, and grace, and comfort, and peace that surpasseth all
understanding.

And, now, do you belong to Christ's Kingdom of Grace?
Does Christ's voice rule your heart? Is He your only
hope and consolation in life and in death? Then these
consoling words apply to you: "Fear not, little flock; for
it is your Father's good pleasure to give you the Kingdom."
For when Christ's loyal subjects die, they pass out of the
world, but remain in His kingdom; from the Kingdom of
Grace they are transferred to His Kingdom of Glory.

3. The Kingdom of Glory.

Of the Kingdom of Glory St. Paul says: *"The Lord
shall deliver me from every evil work and will preserve me
unto His heavenly kingdom: to whom be glory forever
and ever! Amen."*

Smitten down on his way to Damascus, whither he
had gone to hunt and persecute Christians, Paul became
a follower of the lowly Nazarene. Sufferings for the Lord's
sake came to him thick and fast, as every one knows who
is acquainted with the history of his life. Often he was in
danger of losing his life, but the Lord protected him.
Having recounted several such instances, Paul concludes
his second letter to his faithful spiritual son Timothy with
the words: *"The Lord,"* my Savior, whose I am and whom
I serve, *"shall deliver me from every evil work."* He has
done that in the past; He will do it in future. My
enemies, the devil and the world, may concoct "evil works,"
evil plans, against me. In this world we have tribulation.
The Kingdom of Grace is at the same time a kingdom of
the *cross.* But final deliverance will surely come. In spite

of all trials and tribulations here below the King guards and protects His subjects "from every evil work," and we shall and can rest assured with Paul that He *"will preserve us unto His heavenly kingdom."* From the Church Militant the believers are transplanted into the Church Triumphant, from the Kingdom of Grace into the *Kingdom of Glory.* Here "God shall wipe away all tears from their eyes; and there shall be no more death, neither sorrow, nor crying, neither shall there be any more pain; for the former things are passed away." Here the cross, there the crown.

And how great will be that glory which is in store for us? The same Paul, consoling the suffering Christians, writes to the Romans: "I reckon that the sufferings of this present time are not worthy to be compared with the glory which shall be revealed in us"; and St. John says: "Beloved, now are we the sons of God, and it doth not yet appear what we shall be; but we know that, when He shall appear, we shall be like Him; for we shall see Him as He is."

Finally, just one more glimpse into this Kingdom of Glory. "After this," writes St. John in Revelation, "I beheld, and, lo, a great multitude, which no man could number, of all nations, and kindreds, and people, and tongues stood before the throne and before the Lamb, clothed with white robes and palms in their hands, and cried with a loud voice, saying, Salvation to our God, which sitteth upon the throne, and unto the Lamb! . . . And one of the elders answered, saying unto me, What are these which are arrayed in white robes, and whence came they? And I said unto him, Sir, thou knowest. And he said to me, These are they which came out of great tribulation and have washed their robes and made them white in the blood of the Lamb. Therefore are they before the throne of God and serve Him day and night in His temple; and He that sitteth on the throne shall dwell among them. They shall hunger no more, neither thirst any more, neither shall the sun light on them nor any heat. For the Lamb, which is in the midst of the throne, shall feed them and shall lead them unto living fountains of waters; and God shall wipe away all tears from their eyes."

Heavenly Father, keep us steadfast in the faith unto our end for Christ's sake that we may enter Thy glory! Amen.

The Humiliation of Christ.

PHIL. 2, 5—8.
Let this mind be in you which was also in Christ Jesus: who, being in the form of God, thought it not robbery to be equal with God, but made Himself of no reputation and took upon Him the form of a servant and was made in the likeness of men; and being found in fashion as a man, He humbled Himself and became obedient unto death, even the death of the cross.

This passage treats of the humiliation of Christ. It is one of the profoundest passages in the New Testament. For its proper understanding we consult the context and find that it serves a very practical purpose. The Philippians are exhorted to do nothing from motives that would advance the glory of either self or any party or faction in the congregation, "but in lowliness of mind let each esteem other better than themselves. Look not every man on his own things, but every man also on the things of others." This is an exhortation necessary, indeed, for every congregation. Actions on the part of some members flowing from selfish motives or serving the interests of party factions have done great harm in many a congregation. Such was the danger facing the church at Philippi. Hence the exhortation to lowliness of mind, to humility. To enforce it, the example of Christ is adduced: "Let this mind be in you which was also in Christ Jesus." Christ humbled

Himself; follow His example, be humble. This is the scope of the text. Christ is presented as a pattern which we should copy.

In the development of this thought the apostle speaks of the humiliation of Christ and its purpose. And this, under the gracious guidance of the Holy Spirit, will be the subject of this evening's discourse: —

The Humiliation of Christ.

1. The first question to consider is: *Who humbled Himself?* The text says: "Let this mind be in you which was also in Christ Jesus. . . . He humbled Himself." Let us observe this well: Christ Jesus humbled Himself — Christ Jesus, the God-man, this theanthropic person, who possesses a human and a divine nature. So, who is humiliated? The person of Jesus Christ.

2. The next question is: *According to what nature was Jesus humiliated? The divine nature, that is self-evident, cannot be abased and cannot be exalted. The divine nature* is immutable, unchangeable. God is God. "Thou art the same." God is the everlasting "I am." Christ was humiliated according to His human nature. The text is very clear on this point. It reads: "He took upon Himself the form of a servant and was made in the likeness of men; and being found in fashion as a man, He . . . became obedient unto death," all of which can be said only of His human nature.

Again, the very purpose of the apostle makes this clear. The apostle, as we have heard, exhorts to humility. "Let this mind be in you which was also in Christ Jesus" — be humble. According to His divine nature Paul would not and could not present Christ as a pattern, but only according to His human nature.

Of this Christ it is said: He was "in the form of God."

3. *What is the form of God?* The text reads: "Christ

Jesus," the God-man, *"who, being,"* i. e., existing, *"in the form of God, thought it not robbery to be equal with God, but made Himself of no reputation."* What then, is the form of God? *Form* is that by which a person or thing is known or manifested; "form of God," that whereby God is known, seen, or manifested as God; in other words, it is the divine majesty, the divine glory. Externally Christ appeared to be but a man, but He had something about Him to manifest Him as God. In John 2 we are told of His turning water into wine. That was a miracle which only God could perform. Christ thereby manifested Himself as God. In John 11 the climax of Christ's miracles, the raising of Lazarus, is recorded. Christ proved Himself to be God. This man Christ is the almighty God. This the people saw. Thus He was known to be God. This is "the form of God." In this form of God Christ existed. It was His own. "He manifested forth *His glory.*" John 2, 11. When the devil appears as an angel of light, he assumes a form not his own. He assumes a form that does not belong to him. Not so with Christ. When He manifested His glory, His form of God, His divine majesty, it was His own, which He might have used and exhibited at all times. But this He did not do. He possessed this divine majesty at all times. Only a few hours before His death He felled His captors with the simple words: "I am He."

4. *Wherein, then, does this humiliation consist?* "He humbled Himself." How? By taking upon Himself "the form of a servant." What is the form of a servant? Can it be the human nature? No. Why not? The form of a servant Christ laid aside in the state of exaltation. If the human nature were the form of a servant, Christ would no longer be true man — a doctrine which is against all Scripture. Let us follow the text closely. Paul says:

"Christ Jesus," the God-man, this person who possessed not only a divine, but also a human nature, *"took upon Himself the form of a servant."* So the form of a servant is something distinct from the human nature. What does the apostle mean? As the form of God is that whereby God is known, seen, or manifested, so the form of a servant is that whereby Christ is known, seen, or manifested as a servant. Christ, who also according to His human nature possessed all power in heaven and on earth; who also according to His human nature, in the state of humiliation, was the Lord of lords; whom the heavenly hosts would gladly have served at all times, came to *serve* others, to *serve* us, to *redeem* us. This is what the apostle says: *"Let this mind be in you which was also in Christ Jesus."* He existed in the form of God, possessed divine majesty at all times, was equal with God in the state of humiliation; but how was He minded? *"He thought it not robbery to be equal with God."* His being on an equality with God He did not consider a thing to be grasped. He was equal with God, but He did not make a boast, a display, of it; He did not manifest it at all times as He might have done. In ancient times victors paraded their "robbery," *i. e.,* the things they had robbed from the enemy, their booty, their spoils, through the streets in triumph for all to gaze on. What did Christ do? Instead of manifesting Himself as the Lord of man, He manifested Himself as the *servant* of man. This thought of the apostle is further developed: He *"was made in the likeness of men."* He was just like other men, sin excepted. He was a child and grew in wisdom and stature; He was an Israelite among Israelities, a poor peasant among other poor peasants; there was no external mark distinguishing Him from the rest. He was found in fashion as a man. He ate, He drank, He wept, He slept. He, the Son of God, humbled Himself.

Aye, indeed, *He* humbled Himself. *He* did it; it was an act of His, not a fate that had overtaken Him. Voluntarily He did it — for a purpose. Voluntarily, for our sakes, He forewent high stations, honors, and prerogatives which He might rightfully claim and enjoy, being equal with God, very God Himself.

Before passing on to the next point, let us endeavor to deepen our conception of "the form of God" and "the form of a servant." Matt. 8, 23—27 relates Christ's stilling of the tempest on the Sea of Galilee. The ship sets out, the weather is fair, the sea is calm. Tired of the day's labor, Christ "was asleep". Here we see "the form of a servant": He slept. He was *"made in the likeness of men";* like other men He was in need of sleep; He was *"found in fashion as a man."* Suddenly "there arose a great tempest in the sea, insomuch that the ship was covered with the waves." It was a storm the like of which these hardy fishermen, used to all kinds of rough weather, had never before experienced. The danger to that frail craft was exceedingly great; certain death stared the disciples in the face. They despair of their lives. There is but one hope: Christ is in the ship, but—"He was asleep." Crying with a loud voice, "Lord, save us; we perish!" they awaken Him. And "He rebuked the winds and the sea, and there was a great calm." The angry waves were obedient to His will. Here we behold "the form of God." Whenever it pleased Him, He could make use of His divine majesty. The men, marveling, say, "What manner of man is this that even the winds and the sea obey Him!" He is "in the likeness of men," just like other men; yet He must be something greater. He cannot be from the earth, He must be from heaven. They saw the form of God, the majesty of God. They saw He was "equal with God." And it was not robbery on the part of Christ to act as He did, for He was God even in the state of humiliation.

Or take Mark 5, 41 ff. The daughter of Jairus was dead. Christ had said, "The damsel is not dead." "They laughed Him to scorn." He was in fashion as a man; this they saw. The girl was dead; this they knew. Christ brought her to life: "Talitha, cumi!" The sneers were turned into astonishment; they saw "the form of God." Indeed, He was "equal with God." But He did not always manifest it — for a purpose.

5. *What was the purpose of Christ's humiliation?* This is indicated in the words: *"He became obedient* unto *death, even the death of the cross."* This is the last stage of humiliation, the climax of self-humiliation. His agony in the Garden, His capture, the treason of Judas, the denial of Peter, the trial before Caiaphas, Annas, and Pilate, His crucifixion, the whole passion history, is presupposed in the words: "He became obedient unto death, even the death of the cross." So deeply did Christ humble Himself that He died the death of a vile criminal — for us. Why did He die on the cross? Paul says: "Christ hath redeemed us from the curse of the Law, being made a curse for us; for it is written: Cursed is every one that hangeth on a tree." Peter says: "Ye know that ye were not redeemed with corruptible things, as silver and gold, from your vain conversation received by tradition from your fathers, but with the precious blood of Christ, as of a Lamb without blemish and without spot." On the cross He cried out, "It is finished!" All prophecies are fulfilled, the types and shadows of the Ceremonial Law have reached the purpose which they were to serve, the work for which He had been sent to earth in accordance with God's divine decree is at last completed, the penalties allotted to sinners have been endured, redemption is now perfected. The writer of the Epistle to the Hebrews says: "By one offer-

ing He hath perfected forever them that are sanctified."
That was the purpose of His humiliation — our salvation!
That was the reason why He did not constantly employ the
form of God, His divine majesty, which He at all times
possessed. Hence Isaiah exclaims: "Surely He hath borne
our griefs and carried our sorrows; yet we did esteem Him
stricken, smitten of God, and afflicted. But He was
wounded for our transgressions, He was bruised for our
iniquities; the chastisement of our peace was upon Him,
and with His stripes we are healed." The purpose of His
humiliation was to swallow up death in victory that we
might bless God, saying: "Thanks be to God, which giveth
us the victory through our Lord Jesus Christ!" Amen.

Christ's Descent into Hell.

1 PET. 3, 18—20.

For Christ also hath once suffered for sins, the Just for the
unjust, that He might bring us to God, being put to death in the
flesh, but quickened by the Spirit; by which also He went and
preached unto the spirits in prison, which sometime were disobedient, when once the long-suffering of God waited in the days
of Noah, while the ark was a-preparing.

Christ's descent into hell takes a prominent position
in the Second Article of our Christian Creed. It reads:
"I believe in Jesus Christ, His only Son, our Lord, who
was conceived by the Holy Ghost, born of the Virgin Mary,
suffered under Pontius Pilate, was crucified, dead, and
buried; *He descended into hell;* the third day He rose
again from the dead; He ascended into heaven and sitteth
at the right hand of God the Father Almighty, from thence
He shall come to judge the quick and the dead." You
perceive that the various members composing this article

embody great and glorious truths concerning the person of our Savior and His great work of redemption. And, thank God, the import of these members is pretty well understood by Lutheran audiences. The Lutheran Church, more than any other denomination, lays great stress upon the doctrines of the Bible. She endeavors to rear spiritual children well versed in all the counsels of God.

Mostly all the members enumerated in the Second Article, besides being touched upon again and again during the church-year, are such as call for discussion and full presentation on the high festivals of the church-year; hence they are not, or need not be, unknown quantities to our people. What Christian does not know, for example, the doctrine of the person of Christ, or the blessed import of the Passion of Christ, or that of His resurrection, or that of His ascension, or that of His sitting at the right hand of God?

Not so well known, because there is no special Sunday set aside for its consideration, is the doctrine of Christ's descent into hell. This doctrine, however, is so important as to be incorporated into the Christian Creed, together with the other great doctrines concerning our salvation. The words read: *"He,"* Christ, *"descended into hell."* These words mean something. Now, what do they say? They are taken from the first Epistle of St. Peter, chap. 3, 19. Hence a consideration of this passage from Peter will give us the required answer. Peter says: *"For Christ also hath once suffered for sins, the Just for the unjust, that He might bring us to God, being put to death in the flesh, but quickened by the Spirit; by which also He went and preached unto the spirits in prison, which sometime were disobedient, when once the long-suffering of God waited in the days of Noah, while the ark was a-preparing."*

In accordance with this text, the seat of this doctrine, and under the guidance of the Holy Ghost, let us consider:

Christ's Descent into Hell.

We shall treat,

1. Of the person that descended into hell;
2. Of the place whither He descended;
3. Of the time of the descent;
4. Of the purpose of the descent.

1.

Who descended into hell? The text is very explicit. *"For Christ also hath once suffered for sins, . . . being put to death in the flesh, but quickened by the Spirit, by which also He went."* Christ went. And who is Christ? True man, born of the Virgin Mary, and God's Son, true God. Christ is the God-man. This Person, who is at once true man and true God, "went"; the whole Person, with body and soul, "went." It is the same Person who afterwards, as the context says, ascended into heaven. So it is wrong to say, as some do, that this descent took place while Christ's body lay in the grave, and that He performed the work according to His soul only. Let us observe the text closely: *"For Christ,"* that is, the God-man, the whole Person, *"being put to death in the flesh,"* — Christ died according to His human nature, — *"but"* — He did not remain in death — *"quickened by the Spirit,"* that is, made alive by virtue of His divine nature, as He said: "Destroy this temple," meaning His body, "and in three days I will raise it up." So Christ, who suffered and died for us, was quickened, vivified, made alive; body and soul were reunited. This same *Christ,* having finished the work of redemption, and being now in a glorified state, *"went."* No matter to what mystery this may lead us, this is what the text says.

According to which of His two natures did Christ descend into hell? According to His human nature; for as God He is omnipresent and cannot be said to go anywhere. It is He that fills heaven and earth. No, the whole Person went, but according to the human nature. The text is clear also on this point. *"Christ was put to death in the flesh"* (human nature), *"but quickened by the Spirit"* (divine nature); *"by which also He went." "By which,"* His divine nature, in virtue of this divine nature, in the power of this divine nature, He went. On account of the personal union of the two natures in Christ this going to a certain place, which is a property of the one nature only, is predicated of the whole Person. So, then, *Christ the God-man* went to this place, this designated prison.

Now, what are we to understand by this term?

2.

"Christ went and preached to the spirits in prison." Light is shed upon the nature of this place if we read on: Christ went and preached *"to the spirits in prison, which sometime were disobedient in the days of Noah."* This says: At the time of Noah people were disobedient. Disobedient to what? To the Word of God preached to them. They had heard the Gospel, but turned a deaf ear to it, just as so many do to-day. They did not believe. These people perished in the Flood. These disobedient people, dying in unbelief, are now "in prison." Where do unbelieving people go? To hell. This prison is hell. "He that believeth not shall be damned." "Prison" is the abode of the damned — hell.

Scripture teaches throughout its pages that there are but two places hereafter, heaven and hell. To designate this latter place, hell, the New Testament employs three words: hell, Hades, and prison. All three denote the same place — hell. This place, for those dying in unbelief, is called *hell* on account of the fiery tortures there to be endured. The same place is called *Hades,* "the realm of the dead," in reference to *eternal* death. Once in hell, death is everlasting, eternal. Hades is hell. Aye, it is a direct synonym for hell in the New Testament, all the vain mouthings of the modern theologian to the contrary notwithstanding. It does not take great acumen of mind to see this. Luke 16, 23. 24 speaks of the rich man in hell. Our King James Version correctly and plainly renders the text thus: "And in *hell* he [the rich man] lifted up his eyes, being in torments." The Revised Version says: "And in *Hades* he lifted up his eyes." Hades, the modern theologian would have us believe, is a sort of quiet anteroom to heaven, a waiting-room, and, withal, a pretty comfortable place. All this is mere twaddle. Judge for yourselves. Take the text of the Revised Version for the sake of argument. There the text reads: "And *in Hades* he lifted up his eyes, being in torments." So Hades is a place of torments, of excruciating pain. Hades is hell. The text reads on: "And seeth Abraham afar off and Lazarus in his bosom." Abraham and Lazarus were in heaven; the rich man, afar off in that other place, hell; "and he cried and said, Father Abraham, have mercy on me." So the rich man, being in Hades, was in a place where no mercy is shown. Hades is hell. The text proceeds: "And send Lazarus that he may dip the tip of his finger in water and cool my tongue." Such is the nature of this place Hades that the granting of one drop of water to alleviate these terrible torments for the one-thousandth part of a second is looked upon as a great mercy. The rich man goes on to say: "For I am tormented in this flame." Hades is a place where the inmates are tormented in the "flame," in fire. Hades is hell. You see, the King James Version is correct. (*Luther:* "Als er in der Hoelle und in der Qual war.")

The third word the New Testament employs to describe hell is the one in our text, prison. "Prison" this place of torment is called to indicate its purpose. Hell is a prison from which there is no escape. Matt. 5, 26 our Lord Himself speaks of this prison, saying of such as enter it: "Verily, I say unto thee, Thou shalt by no means come out thence till thou hast paid the uttermost farthing." When will that be? Never. Thus "hell," "Hades," and "prison" all denote one and the same place, that place "which is prepared for the devil and his angels"; that place of which, in reference to the unbelievers, it is said: "Their worm shall not die, neither shall their fire be quenched; and they shall be an abhorring to all flesh." To this place Christ went.

3.

When did He go? That question is easily answered by consulting the text. On the cross Christ had cried out, "It is finished." The work of redemption was completed. Hence the text says: "Christ once suffered for sins, the Just for the unjust, being put to death in the flesh, but quickened by the Spirit; by which also He went and preached to the spirits in prison." He was put to death, then quickened, *i. e.,* vivified, made alive; then He went to the prison, *i. e.,* He descended into hell; next followed His resurrection, then His ascension. So the time is clearly marked. It was after His quickening and before His resurrection. In that interval, perhaps in a moment of time, the now glorified Christ appeared in the nether world.

4.

What was His purpose in going there? The text answers: *"To preach,"* to preach to the spirits in prison. In spite of this plain, unmistakable assertion there are such as teach that Christ descended into hell to suffer the torments of hell for us. This is absolutely false. It does not only do violence to this text, but it is contrary to the words of our Savior uttered on the cross, "It is finished." Nor was Christ's purpose in descending into hell to release

the Old Testament saints from "prison," as the papists
aver. He went there to preach.

What did He preach? There are such as say that He
preached the Gospel in order to give those who had no
opportunity to hear it in this life another chance to hear
of, and accept, the merits of Christ and thus be saved.
Absolutely false again, for the text says plainly: Christ
preached to such as *"sometime were disobedient,"* who
would not believe. These people, during their lifetime,
heard the Gospel, but they would not believe. This thought,
that Christ preached the Gospel in hell, sprung from the
fertile imagination of some German theologians, was later
expanded, and the possibility of conversion after death for
all was taught. This doctrine, which is but the doctrine
of purgatory of the Catholics, furbished and polished up
somewhat, has no foundation in Scripture, as even some
of the most noted leaders who promulgate this dogma
honestly concede; but the thought is fascinating to them,
and thus they teach "commandments," or rather figments,
"of men as doctrines of God." It is a soul-destroying
doctrine, which fosters carnal security. It is a religion of
the flesh. People are led to think: "Well and good, it
matters not how I live and die; after death I'll have another
chance of being saved, and I'll be sure to embrace it."

Oh, how much these seducers of souls will have to
answer for on that Great Day! For it is written: "It is
appointed unto men once to die, but after this" — what?
A millennium? No. A state of second probation? No.
A possibility of conversion? No! a thousand times No! —
"but after this the Judgment." There is no conversion
after death. "He that believeth and is baptized shall be
saved, but he that believeth not shall be damned." And
what does the story of the rich man and poor Lazarus
teach? We read: "The rich man died and was buried."
And the very next thing? "And in hell he lifted up his

eyes, being in torments." No conversion after death. "He that believeth not is condemned already because he hath not believed in the name of the only-begotten Son of God."

All Scripture, as you see, is against this doctrine of a second probation, and those who hold it get no consolation from our text. Nowhere does it say here that Christ preached the Gospel. It simply says: *"He preached."* The word in the original is a word of neutral meaning, which, translated, means to preach, to proclaim, to publish as a herald. This is conceded by all conversant with the matter.

How, then, do we know what Christ did preach? The context must give us the key to that. And here the context is plain, forceful, cogent, so that any one open to conviction, who investigates it with an unbiased mind, without preconceived opinions, cannot be left in doubt as to its meaning. Christ preached the Law, the damning Law. He told those to whom He preached: "You are justly damned!" Let us see that. *"Christ preached to the spirits in prison, which sometime were disobedient, when once the long-suffering of God waited in the days of Noah, while the ark was a-preparing."* That is the text. What does it say? These people were "disobedient." The Gospel had been preached to them during their lifetime. They despised it. "He that believeth not shall be damned." This Christ preached to them. "You have despised Me, therefore your lot is just." God was "long-suffering once," during their lifetime; now this long-suffering had come to an end. God "waited." He had waited 120 years. God had given them a long time to repent. They would not. God had done everything to save them: He had sent them the preacher of righteousness, Noah, to warn them of their impending doom if they would not turn; the building of the ark itself was an object-sermon. They despised Noah and ridiculed the building of the ark. Thus we see, the guilt, the damning guilt, of these people is stressed. And the correlative of guilt is punishment. If the modern theologians were right, who say that the Gospel was preached to them, we should at least expect a mitigating circumstance, an excuse for their disobedience; but we find nothing of the kind. Their guilt is emphasized, and guilt demands punishment. Whosoever despises the grace of God, rejects the grace of God, must be punished. The doctrine taught here is: Unbelief is the cause of damnation. So, then, it was not the Gospel which Christ preached, but the Law, the Judgment. The exact words are not given, but the import of His sermon was: "You have despised Me, whom you now see to be the Victor over death and hell and sin; you are justly damned." That is the sermon that all damned must hear to all eternity. Christ, the Savior, has no other message for them when the accepted time, in this world, the day of salvation, has been neglected.

Thus Christ showed Himself to the infernal spirits as the Conqueror of the devil, of hell, and all hellish foes, and mightily triumphed over them. He has, as we read in Colossians (2, 15), "spoiled principalities and powers" and "made a show of them openly, triumphing over them." And the psalmist exclaims: "Thou hast led captivity captive; Thou hast received gifts for men, yea, for the rebellious also, that the Lord might dwell among them." And Hosea says: "Death, I will be thy plague; O hell, I will be thy destruction!"

Had Christ not descended into hell, the anxious question might arise in our hearts: "It is true, Christ has cried out on the cross, 'It is finished'; but did He really overcome our great foe, Satan?" Now, however, the joyful answer is: "Yes. By His death Christ vanquished the devil; by His descent into hell He made that fact patent to the devil, 'I am the Victor'; by His resurrection He proclaimed His victory to men; by His ascension into heaven He announced it to the angels."

Thus the doctrine of Christ's descent into hell makes us all the more sure of this glorious truth, "that Jesus Christ, true God, begotten of the Father from eternity, and also true man, born of the Virgin Mary, is my Lord, who has redeemed me, purchased and won me, from death and from the power of the devil."

May God in His mercy grant that we apply also this doctrine for our consolation now and in the hour of death, apply it for our souls' salvation! Amen.

The Resurrection of Jesus Christ.

Rom. 1, 1—4.

Paul, a servant of Jesus Christ, called to be an apostle, . . . concerning His Son Jesus Christ, our Lord, which was made of the seed of David according to the flesh and declared to be the Son of God with power, according to the Spirit of Holiness, by the resurrection from the dead.

The resurrection of Jesus Christ from the dead is the corner-stone of the Christian religion. Disprove it, and Christianity collapses. Too well was and is this truth known by Satan and all his hellish cohorts. From the beginning of the Christian era to this day the enemies of Christ have busied themselves to disprove this miracle of miracles — His resurrection from the dead. But vain have been all their attempts, and vain will they be to the end of time.

The Christian in whose heart God has mercifully implanted faith, and who therefore can triumphantly exclaim with Job, "I know that my Redeemer liveth," laughs at the impotent rage of Satan and his helpers to storm this citadel of the Christian Church, but pities the poor deluded wretches, who, though they have eyes, see not, and though they have ears, hear not, the things that pertain to their salvation.

For one seeking historic evidences no other fact of history is so well authenticated as the resurrection of Jesus Christ, and by men who knew the facts, could tell the truth, would tell the truth, and for whom the telling of the truth brought nothing but dishonor and persecution.

"Christ showed Himself alive after His Passion by many infallible proofs, being seen of them [the apostles] forty days," writes St. Luke in the Acts. May it suffice this evening simply to enumerate the "infallible proofs," without going into details. He appeared to the grief-stricken Mary Magdalene; He greeted the holy women on their way from the vacant tomb. In the evening of that day He joined Cleopas and another disciple going to Emmaus. Somewhat later He stood in the midst of His disciples, saying, "Peace be unto you!" About a week after, He upbraided Thomas for refusing credible testimony. Next He was seen by above five hundred brethren in Galilee. He was seen of James; He showed Himself to the apostles at the Sea of Tiberias, directing Peter to feed the flock. His last bodily appearance was on Mount Olivet, where He uttered the Great Commission: "Go ye into all the world and preach the Gospel to every creature." Ascending on high, He received gifts for men and on the Day of Pentecost proved to men on earth His enthronement in the heavens.

How thinking men, despite all these cumulative evidences, can still doubt the resurrection of Jesus Christ is hard to comprehend. In their hardness of heart they will not believe. The resurrection of Jesus Christ is an absolute certainty. Oh, what comforting truth that the corner-stone of our Christian religion cannot be removed! God's infallible Word assures us thereof.

Why Is the Resurrection of Christ So Comforting?

Because it is conclusive evidence

1. *That Christ is the Son of God, and that His doctrine is the truth;*
2. *That God has accepted the sacrifice of His Son for the reconciliation of the world;*
3. *That all believers shall arise to eternal life.*

1.

The text speaks of *"Jesus Christ, our Lord, which was made of the seed of David according to the flesh and declared to be the Son of God with power, according to the Spirit of Holiness, by the resurrection from the dead."* Observe the language of the text. Jesus Christ was the Son of God, true God, before the foundation of the world. In time He *"was made of the seed of David according to the flesh"* — He became true man. This God-man, Jesus Christ, in the state of humiliation, proved Himself to be the Son of God by many miracles. He stilled the tempest, cleansed the lepers, raised the widow's son, called Lazarus from the grave, etc. The people saw again and again: this man is true God. But nowhere else, says Paul in our text, have we such conclusive evidence of His being what He claimed to be — Son of God — as in His resurrection from the dead. By that act, as by no other, He was declared to be the powerful, majestic Son of God.

Christ Himself pointed to His resurrection as the greatest proof of His divinity. One day the Jews demanded a special sign of Him as a proof for His Messiahship. "Destroy this temple," said He, meaning His body, "and in three days I will raise it up." What a stupendous assertion to make! For ages and ages generations had come and gone, but from the grave not a single person had returned. And here stands this man Jesus before the

Jews, saying: "You will kill Me, but I shall return from the grave, and I shall rise by My own power. I am the Conqueror of death." What happens? He was crucified, dead, and buried, but on the third day, according to His prediction, He rose again. He spoke truly when He said: I will raise up My body. He spoke truly when He said on another occasion: "I have power to lay down My life, and I have power to take it again." John 10, 18. None but God is the Lord over death. Christ conquered death. He arose of His own power; Christ therefore is God.

But there is another truth in this passage pertinent to the matter in hand. Christ had prophesied His death: "Destroy this temple," My body. He foreknew what the Jews would do with His body — they would "destroy it," kill Him; and He plainly tells them so. He prophesied concerning His resurrection: "In three days I will raise it up." Both prophecies came true. Christ is a true Prophet; His doctrine is the truth. — The resurrection of Christ provides us with a solid foundation for our faith in the divinity of Christ and gives us absolute assurance of the reliability of His doctrine. Now we know with absolute certainty that the Bible is *God's* Word. We can rely upon its every word.

But the resurrection of Jesus Christ does not only prove that Christ is the Son of God, and that His doctrine is the truth, but also that God the Father has accepted the sacrifice of His Son for the reconciliation of the world.

2.

The text says that *"Jesus Christ, our Lord, was made of the seed of David according to the flesh."* These words are very significant. *"Christ was made of the seed of David,"* He became true man — for a purpose. *"David's seed"* was the promised Messiah, who was to deliver all mankind from the wrath of God by suffering and death.

To this fact also His names point, Jesus meaning Savior; Christ, the Anointed. He was anointed to be our Prophet to teach the way of salvation; to be our High Priest, who was to sacrifice Himself in our stead; to be our King, to rule over us here and in eternity. And by His high-priestly office, by suffering and dying for us, He was to win us from the kingdom of Satan and thus become our Lord. And Him who set out to do that very thing God raised from the dead. What does that prove? That God the Father, the Judge, has accepted the sacrifice of His Son for the reconciliation of the world, or as St. Paul puts it: "Christ was delivered for our offenses and was raised again for our justification."

Look at the situation. Christ was our Substitute. The Just, Christ, took the place of the unjust, and the Just "was delivered," given up, to death on account of our trespasses. The Just died for the unjust in order to expiate their sins. And willingly "Christ gave Himself for us that He might redeem us from all iniquity." On the cross at Calvary our Substitute expired with the words on His lips, "It is finished." Atonement for our sins was made. But the anxious question remained, Will God accept this atonement? A dead Savior can avail us nothing. Where is the proof that God is satisfied with the work of His Son?

Sad, sad beyond expression, were our lot if Christ were not risen. St. Paul draws this gloomy picture: "If Christ be not raised, your faith is vain"; your faith has no ground on which to stand, no truth on which to rely. "Ye are yet in your sins." If Christ is not risen, reconciliation with God is not effected, His wrath abideth on you, you have no forgiveness of sin, you are not redeemed. "Then they also which are fallen asleep in Christ are perished." These Christians died in the faith of Christ as their Savior; they believed their death to be but a sleep, after which there would be a joyful awakening. But, lo! if Christ be not

raised, they were deluded, then they died without expiation
of their sins and, accordingly, are lost, damned. Aye,
indeed, "if in this life only we have hope in Christ, we are
of all men most miserable." "But," the apostle proceeds,
"now *is* Christ risen from the dead." Hence it follows that
our faith is not vain, but rests upon a firm foundation; our
sins are atoned for. Our Substitute triumphantly arose
from the grave on the third day. "He was raised for our
justification." Here is proof, positive proof, that His
death has been accepted as an expiation for our sins. We
look to Calvary, and we know: "Christ was delivered for
our offenses." We look into the empty grave of Christ
and are assured: "He was raised again for our justification." God the Father has accepted the sacrifice of His
Son for the reconciliation of the world. Hence the great
stress on the fact of the resurrection in our text: *"Jesus
Christ was made of the seed of David according to the
flesh and declared to be the Son of God with power, according to the Spirit of Holiness, by the resurrection from the
dead."* Do you anxiously ask, Will God forgive my sins?
Where are they? In the grave. Christ died for you.
Christ rose for you. Therefore you are free. But accept
this in faith, and the deed is done.

But the resurrection of Christ does not only prove that
Christ is the Son of God, that His doctrine is the truth,
and that God has accepted the sacrifice of His Son for
the reconciliation of the world, but it furthermore assures
us that all believers shall arise to eternal life.

3.

This comforting truth, which elsewhere in the Scriptures is taught in such plain words, is also implied in our
text. The text says that *"Jesus Christ, our Lord, was
declared to be the Son of God with power by the resurrection from the dead."* What does this say? In the state

of humiliation Christ at all times was the mighty God, but He did not always appear as such: He did not always use His divine majesty and power, communicated to His human nature by virtue of the personal union; now, however, by and since His resurrection, He is declared to be the Son of God *with power,* the powerful, majestic Son of God; now, in the state of exaltation, He fully and constantly uses the divine majesty communicated to His human nature also according to His human nature; now He sits at the right hand of God, where He, our Brother, mightily rules over all our spiritual enemies and finally, when this life's strife is over, will lead us to the heavenly mansions prepared for us. He surely will make His promise true: "Where I am, there shall also My servant be" — in glory.

To illustrate this consoling truth, allow me to take you into a little Christian family in the small village at Bethany. Here deep sorrow reigns. Martha and Mary mourn over the death of their brother Lazarus. Jesus comes that way, and in the course of the conversation He consoles Martha by saying: "Thy brother shall rise again." Martha believes that. She says: "I know he shall rise again in the resurrection at the Last Day." Then Jesus utters these mighty words: "I am the Resurrection," and hence the whole power to effect it is Mine. In Me the resurrection is absolutely certain. I am "the Life." I have immortality, imperishable, unchanging life, in Myself and can impart it to others, so they need not and cannot die. "He that believeth in Me, though He were dead, yet shall he live." Belief in Me, faith in Me, so intimately unites the believer with Me that, as certainly as I live, the believer shall also live. — "Because I live, ye shall live also." True, the Christian, too, must die. But in the light of Scripture, what is temporal death for the Christian? A sleep. Says Paul: "If we believe that

Jesus died and rose again, even so them also which sleep in Jesus will God bring with Him"; and Jesus says: "Verily, verily, I say unto you, If a man keep My saying, he shall never see death." The bitterness of death the Christian shall not taste. Death to him is but a sleep, after which there is a blissful awakening. Death has been swallowed up of Life. The temporal death of Christians is so little to be regarded as death that Christ says: "And whosoever liveth and believeth in Me shall never die." Temporal death to the Christians is but an entrance into eternal life. — Thus the resurrection of Christ from the dead makes us absolutely certain of a blessed life beyond the grave.

Now, my Christian friend, you are His servant, you believe in Jesus, the risen Savior; why, then, be downcast and mourn? This life with all its sorrows is but as a handbreadth. Soon it will be over, and you will be with the Lord always. Hence imprint indelibly upon the tablets of your heart that "Jesus Christ, our Lord, was made of the seed of David according to the flesh and declared to be the Son of God with power, according to the Spirit of Holiness, by the resurrection from the dead."

Knowing that Christ is the Son of God, and that His doctrine is the truth; knowing that God the Father has accepted the sacrifice of His Son for the reconciliation of the world; knowing that all believers shall rise to eternal life, you can joyfully exclaim with Peter: "Blessed be the God and Father of our Lord Jesus Christ, which according to His abundant mercy hath begotten us again unto a lively hope by the resurrection of Jesus Christ from the dead, to an inheritance incorruptible, undefiled, and that fadeth not away, reserved in heaven for you, who are kept by the power of God through faith unto salvation, ready to be revealed in the last time." This is most certainly true. Amen.

The Joyful Easter Sermon of the Angel in the Grave of Our Lord.

MARK 16, 1—8.

And when the Sabbath was past, Mary Magdalene and Mary, the mother of James, and Salome had bought sweet spices that they might come and anoint Him. And very early in the morning, the first day of the week, they came unto the sepulcher at the rising of the sun. And they said among themselves, Who shall roll us away the stone from the door of the sepulcher? And when they looked, they saw that the stone was rolled away; for it was very great. And entering into the sepulcher, they saw a young man sitting on the right side, clothed in a long white garment; and they were affrighted. And he saith unto them, Be not affrighted. Ye seek Jesus of Nazareth, which was crucified; He is risen; He is not here. Behold the place where they laid Him. But go your way, tell His disciples and Peter that He goeth before you into Galilee; there shall ye see Him, as He said unto you. And they went out quickly and fled from the sepulcher, for they trembled and were amazed; neither said they anything to any man, for they were afraid.

In proclaiming the glorious tidings of His good will toward men, God has at sundry times availed Himself of the ministrations of angels.

To-day I would remind you of but two notable communications made by angels to men. The first of these communications or, I should rather say, sermons — for such they were — was published in that holy night on the plains of Bethlehem to the shepherds keeping watch over their flocks; the other sermon is the one related in our text.

The Christmas sermon read: "Be not afraid; for, behold, I bring you good tidings of great joy, which shall be to all people; for unto you is born this day, in the city of David, a Savior, which is Christ the Lord." And soon the multitude of the heavenly host had assembled, and the still air was filled with celestial strains of "Glory to God in the highest, and on earth peace, good will toward men."

The Easter sermon reads: "Be not afraid; ye seek Jesus of Nazareth, which was crucified; He is not here; He is risen. Behold the place where they laid Him."

The Christmas-sermon was delivered during the night; but this dark night was made brilliant by the glory of the Lord, which shone round about the shepherds, symbolizing, as it were, the result this proclamation should bring about — that of illuminating the dense night of spiritual darkness hovering over the whole world.

The Easter-sermon was published in a grave; and this grave, too, was rendered transcendent beyond description by the brightness of the visitors from above, making it apparent that now even that most dreaded abode, the grave, was divested of its terrors.

The Christmas-sermon was preached at the beginning of Christ's earthly career, when He "was made of a woman, made under the Law, that He might redeem them that were under the Law"; the Easter-sermon, on the other hand, when the work of redemption had been completed, after Christ had spoken the words on the cross, "It is finished!" and when the Father had affixed His divine seal of approval to the work of His Son.

Weighing these two angelic sermons in the balance, which contains the greater, the more important, the more joyful news? Idle question! Both are fraught with joyful news too deep for us to fathom.

Moreover, when the Christmas-anthem was sung by the angelic choir, in the sight of God the Easter-message we hear proclaimed to-day was already a reality, and again without the Easter-message, "He is risen!" the Christmas-tidings, which speak of great joy for all people because of the birth of the Babe at Bethlehem, would be meaningless.

These two sermons are like beautiful, brilliant gems lying side by side in a casket. It is very hard to give the preference to either. So, then, as during Christmas we considered the song of the angels, so let us now, in this joyous Easter-tide, hear

The Joyful Easter-Sermon of the Angel in the Grave of Our Lord.

It contains

1. *An admonition, "Be not affrighted."*
2. *A proclamation of the resurrection, "He is risen; He is not here."*
3. *A command, "Go, tell His disciples and Peter."*

1.

"And when the Sabbath was past, Mary Magdalene and Mary, the mother of James, and Salome had bought sweet spices that they might come and anoint Him. And very early in the morning, the first day of the week, they came unto the sepulcher at the rising of the sun." Vv. 1. 2.

How simple these words, yet how full of meaning! It is Easter-morning. The golden sun is just about to rise in the east and to cast his first faint beams over the city of Jerusalem. The tragedy that had occurred only a few days ago seems to be forgotten. The city is wrapped in peaceful slumber. But some sleep not. At the break of day, "very early," our text says, three women may be seen wending their way to the Lord's sepulcher. Who are they? Mary Magdalene, Mary, the mother of James, and Salome. The two Marys had been under the cross, they had seen their Master expire; and when He was laid to rest by those two secret disciples, Joseph and Nicodemus, love towards their Lord impelled them to be near and view the place where He was laid. In these pathetic words the evangelist describes their love for Jesus: "And Mary Magdalene was there and the other Mary, sitting over against the sepulcher."

And now these two Marys, in company with Salome, are again on their journey to the grave. For them the Lord is dead. They have spices to anoint His dead body.

Who can describe the heartrending sorrow of these women in that hour? They know that the Just and Holy One has been put to death, He who had been their dearest friend, He who had been their Joy, their Peace, their All! How must Mary Magdalene have felt, the great sinner, whom He had forgiven all her sins! And how much had He been to Mary, the mother of James, and to Salome, the mother of the two apostles James and John!

And now He was dead, and they were on the way to His grave.

And what had been their expectation concerning Him? That He would save Israel! And now He was dead! With bowed heads and sealed lips they silently pursue their journey, each occupied with sorrowful thoughts. Grief oftentimes is so deep that it cannot find expression in words. So it was here.

Let us pause and reflect. In these three women we see our own image. We are wanderers, one and all, to the grave. There are graves to the right of us, graves to the left of us. Death flourishes his scepter over all. The summons will come to every one sooner or later to join the innumerable caravan that moves to the realm of the grave. What a gap death often makes in our lives! The nearest and dearest are taken from us with a seemingly ruthless hand. The wife must leave the husband, the husband is separated from the wife, and the lovely child, upon whom we have set our hopes and affections, must be laid under the cool sod. With bowed heads and downcast eyes we follow mourning to the grave, and oftentimes the question rises in our hearts, "Why is this thus? Why, Lord, must it be so?"

"And they said among themselves, Who shall roll us away the stone from the door of the sepulcher? And when they looked, they saw that the stone was rolled away, for it was very great. And entering into the sepulcher, they saw a young man sitting on the right side, clothed in a long white garment; and they were affrighted. And he said unto them, Be not afraid." Vv. 3—6.

Upon approaching the sepulcher, the women with an effort dispel their somber musings and turn to practical questions, "Who shall roll us away the stone from the door of the sepulcher?" Fortunately they had not thought of that before, nor of the seal affixed to the stone, nor about the guard that had been stationed at the grave. They must anoint Him, and they must cast one last, long, lingering look upon the dead body of their Master! These thoughts filled their hearts. And the stone and the seal and the guard did not once occur to their minds. Fortunately, otherwise they might have been deterred from coming at all.

How true to life! How often do we not walk blind-folded, as it were! Love to our Lord prompts us to do this or that; we see not the great obstacles in our way, and, lo! when after sober second thoughts these insur-mountable obstacles present themselves to our mind, God has removed them. So here. Lifting up their eyes, the women observe from a distance that the great stone is rolled away. Picture to yourselves their amazement on beholding this. They know something unusual must have happened. Boldly, though trembling and fearing, they enter the grave. But how is their perplexity heightened when, not finding the Lord's body, they, of a sudden, see a young man sitting at the right side, clothed in a long white garment. "His countenance," says Matthew, "was like lightning and His raiment white as snow."

Contemplate this grave. It is empty! The door is

open. It is not a dark, deep dungeon, but lit up by the glory of the Lord. Why, this is not the realm of death!

And the women were amazed. Small wonder. But the angel of the Lord — for such was that young man in the white garment — immediately silences their fears. "Be not affrighted!" says he. You are in a grave, but — "be not affrighted!"

Wonderful, joyful Easter-message! It is calculated to take away all dread from the abode of the dead.

Where are most tears shed? At the coffin and the grave. Of what nature are those thoughts that make men shudder? Thoughts of the grave and of death, thoughts of the shroud and the pall. And here these women are bidden, "Be not affrighted!" In the environments of death you are; still, fear not!

Indeed, a joyous Easter-message if such words issue from the grave. What, then, is the key? It is this, "Fear not *ye*" — and the angel lays particular stress upon the word *"ye,"* as if to say: Those others, the guards of the sepulcher, the enemies of Christ, have need to fear and tremble, but ye, ye lovers of the Lord, fear not ye, "be not affrighted!"

And now, my friends, as we stand around the grave of our loved ones and contemplate our own end of life, there comes from the grave this tender message, "Fear not!" For you the grave has lost its terrors. Your grave, too, is lit up by the brightness of the Lord. It is not the dark place so commonly pictured. The grave does not end all. Triumphantly we may sing in bold defiance, "O grave, where is thy victory?" And as we listen to the words of the minister over the grave, words of consolation and hope and peace, we know that he is but doing what the angel did here; he is saying, "Fear not ye."

And why all this? That we shall learn from the proclamation of the resurrection.

2.

*"Ye seek Jesus of Nazareth, which was crucified. He
is risen; He is not here. Behold the place where they
laid Him,"* v. 6.

I know your mission, says the angel; you are lovers
of the Lord Jesus, whom you know to be the Messiah, the
Savior, but who is so despised that He is called the Nazarene. Though others despise Him, you despise Him not;
your love to Him prompted you to come here in spite of
the danger of death from the Jews, who hated Him and
therefore also hate you.

But why are you so slow of heart to believe all that
Moses and the prophets have said concerning Him? "Why
seek ye the living among the dead?" Luke 24, 5. He is
not here; but still He has not been carried away to another
place as a corpse, His body has not been stolen; no, "He
is risen!" He is risen by His own power; "He lives," as
He said. Investigate every nook and corner of the sepulcher, convince yourselves of the truth of my words; "behold
the place where they laid Him"; He *"was* crucified," but
that scene is now past. He is risen, and thereby He has
declared Himself with power the Son of God.

It is well-nigh impossible to describe the feelings of
the women on hearing this joyful Easter-message. Matthew
says that they were filled with fear and joy. Joy may some-
times be so great, so overwhelming, so bewildering, that
one cannot believe one's own senses. So it was here. We
have accompanied these women on the way to the grave,
and have listened, as it were, to their inmost thoughts.
Surely this is the Messiah, they said to themselves. Had
He not often told them so; had He not proved His divine
mission and His divinity? But now He lay in the grave.
Now He was dead, so they thought. Now all had come to
an end. The mystery of it all was too deep for them
to fathom.

But now they hear the joyful news, "He was crucified, but He is risen!" Now the Scriptures were opened unto them. He was crucified, but now He lives. Why, had He not often spoken to them in a most sublime way of the death that He would suffer? Had He not said regarding His disciples: "The days will come when the Bridegroom shall be taken from them"? Had He not said: "Behold, we go up to Jerusalem, and all things that are written by the prophets concerning the Son of Man shall be accomplished; for He shall be delivered unto the Gentiles, and shall be mocked, and spitefully entreated, and spitted on; and they shall scourge Him and put Him to death; and the third day He shall rise again"? Why had they not thought of that and believed? Had He not said, in cleansing the Temple of its unholy and desecrating traders: "Destroy this temple, and in three days I will raise it up"? Now these words had come true. Now was the third day. These and many other things came back to their minds like a flash. Ah, indeed, He was the Messiah! Awe-inspiring and sublime news at once. Small wonder they were filled with fear and joy.

And what was the import of it all? Let Paul answer: "He was delivered for our offenses and raised again for our justification." Now, "who shall lay anything to the charge of God's elect? It is God that justifieth." What was the import? Hear Peter: "Blessed be the God and Father of our Lord Jesus Christ, which according to His abundant mercy hath begotten us again unto a lively hope by the resurrection of Jesus Christ from the dead, to an inheritance incorruptible, and undefiled, and that fadeth not away, reserved in heaven for you who are kept by the power of God through faith unto salvation." As our Substitute He had entered death, defied the devil and all our foes. He has conquered and thus brought life and immortality to light. Our Substitute is free, and so we are free. The handwriting that was against us is blotted out by the hands of God the Father. "If Christ be not raised, your faith is vain, ye are yet in your sins." But Christ is raised, and your faith is not vain, and ye who believe are not in your sins.

Come, sinner, to the empty grave of Christ and read your pardon there.

But more than that. "Christ is risen from the dead and become the First-fruits of them that sleep." His resurrection is proof of our own. "He is not here, He is risen," was said to the women. And so one day it will be said of each one of us who have believed in Him: "He is not here, he is risen." And what shall become of us? Job answers: "I know that my Redeemer liveth; . . . and though, after my skin, worms destroy this body, yet in my flesh shall I see God." Yes, in this my flesh shall I see God; but this flesh, like the body of Christ, will be in a glorious condition, in a glorious state; for, says St. Paul, "the Lord Jesus Christ shall change our vile body that it may be fashioned like unto His glorious body."

So come, my Christian friends, and look into the grave of Christ once more. It is empty; so yours one day will be empty. Of Christ it was said, "He is not here, He is risen"; likewise of you it will be said, "He is not here, he is risen." There is a rising after death, just as there is a rising after sleep. Do you fear sleep? No. Then fight down in the armor of God that terror of the grave and view your grave in the light of the Easter-message as your "cemetery," as your sleeping-chamber, hallowed by Christ. Fear not! Your soul will be carried into Abraham's bosom, and on the Latter Day body and soul will be reunited, and you shall be with the Lord always in those heavenly mansions which He has prepared for you.

Oh, for the joyful news of this Easter-sermon of the angel in the grave! To whom does it apply?

3.

"Go your way," says the angel to the women. Out of love you have brought sweet spices to anoint your dear Master, but, as you see, love's labor's lost. There is no need for that; do something better: *"Tell His disciples."*

Oh, for the great love of the Savior! But perhaps the disciples deserved to have this glorious news made known unto them? No, no! Each and every one had proved faithless. In the hour of Jesus' greatest need when He was taken captive, and when His disciples should have quitted themselves like men, we read: "Then all His disciples left Him and fled." This cowardly flight on the part of the disciples was a great sin. They believed that He was Jesus, the Son of God. Christ, moreover, had told them beforehand how everything should come to pass, and still they fled. He had taught them for three years with all diligence, and still they proved faithless — they fled. They sinned against better knowledge. And when Christ was on the cross, where were His disciples? Under the cross, perhaps, standing by their Master to the last bitter end? No, again; one disciple only, he "whom He loved," was there; the rest were women.

Where were the disciples? Behind closed doors! Surely these disciples had deserved to be cast away. "Tell the world of My resurrection, but not these My one-time disciples!" — had this command been given to the angel, it would have served those faithless disciples right. But behold the love of the Savior! These very same men who had deserted Him in the hour of anguish, these men who had secured themselves behind barred doors out of fear of the Jews, these men should be told, "He is risen!" Why? They, most of all, were in need of comfort; they must know that they have a living Savior, that He had died for their sins, and was risen again for their justification.

And what these women were bidden to do, that, too, is my blessed privilege this evening. The command, "Tell His disciples," is valid to this day.

Have you been a disciple of the Lord, and have you also proved faithless? I am bidden to tell you that the Savior will not cast you away. Think but of these faithless disciples, and as truly as He received them, He will also receive you.

"But," you say, "all good and well; that may be joyful news for some, but my sins are like scarlet; I am past hope."

No, my friend, I shall not allow you to escape. Come to Jesus; He is calling you. Hear what the text says and believe: "Tell My disciples *and Peter.*" Why is the addition made, "and Peter"? Peter was a disciple, why, then, mention his name expressly? Why not simply say, "Tell My disciples"? That would include Peter. No, the Lord knew better. Peter was most in need of this Easter-message, and he would be the very one, most likely, who, on hearing the message proclaimed in a general way, would exclude himself and say, "Good news for you, my fellow-disciples, but it is not intended for me; my sins are too great and too many."

Peter had fallen more deeply than the rest. At the first trial of Jesus, Peter was standing at the fire warming himself, and when he was asked, "Art thou also one of His disciples?" he denied with an oath and said, "I am not." And after the space of an hour, being again asked as to his discipleship, he began to curse and swear, "I know not this man of whom ye speak." This was the same Peter who a little while before had been ready, as he said, to die with the Lord. Peter, Peter, you knew who your Master was! You made a good confession once upon a time when you said to Jesus, "Thou art the Christ, the Son of the living God." And now with a gesture of contempt you say,

"I know not this man!" Peter, you have deserved to be cast away. But the Lord is full of mercy and forgiveness, too deep for us to comprehend. Tell this great sinner, Peter, is the command, that "He is risen!" Do not forget Peter!

And now, my friend, whoever you are, and if you are a Peter who has denied his Lord — the Savior's love towards you is so great that He bids me tell you that He will not cast you away. He accepted Peter, He will accept you. Be not unbelieving, but believing, and thank and praise the Lord for His mercy.

And if, perchance, there are some here this evening who never have tasted that the Lord is good, who never have been His disciples, you, too, the Lord bids come. For if He accepted His faithless disciples and Peter, He surely will accept you, who never as yet have been His followers. Simply believe the Easter-message, and though it may seem too great news to you, appropriate it unto yourselves nevertheless and rejoice with all true Christians over this Easter-sermon from the grave. In Christ's name we bid you, Come! He says: "Him that cometh to Me I will in no wise cast out." Therefore answer: —

> Just as I am, without one plea,
> But that Thy blood was shed for me,
> And that Thou bidst me come to Thee,
> O Lamb of God, I come, I come!

> Just as I am, Thy love unknown
> Has broken every barrier down;
> Now to be Thine, yea, Thine alone,
> O Lamb of God, I come, I come!

Amen.

Christ's Sitting at the Right Hand of God.

EPH. 1, 20—23.

God set Him at His own right hand in the heavenly places, far above all principality, and power, and might, and dominion, and every name that is named, not only in this world, but also in that which is to come; and hath put all things under His feet; and gave Him to be the Head over all things to the Church, which is His body, the fulness of Him that filleth all in all.

The paragraph of which our text forms the close, contains a supplication of St. Paul for the Christians at Ephesus. It is replete with consolation and encouragement for the Christians and the Christian Church. Our text speaks of the Church, of its security. We often tremble for its welfare. We observe the high winds and the angry waves of adversity coming threateningly upon the ship of the Church and forget the nearness of the Lord. A thorough knowledge of what this means: Christ sits at the right hand of God, and a childlike faith in that truth will dispel our fears. Instead of crying out in consternation with the disciples on the tempest-tossed Galilean sea: "Lord, save us; we perish!" a prayerful study of this text will make us bold triumphantly and defiantly to challenge all adversaries with Paul: "If God be for us, who can be against us?"

St. Paul prays God that the Ephesian Christians may have the eyes of their hearts enlightened, so that they may know, among other things, also this, what is the power of Him who sitteth at the right hand of God, and what His relation is to the Church. This knowledge will afford them great consolation.

The Sitting of Christ at the Right Hand of God a Strong Consolation for His Members.

For

1. *Christ is the Ruler of the universe;*
2. *Christ is the Head of the Church.*

1.

After His resurrection from the dead, Christ "showed Himself alive to His disciples by many infallible proofs, being seen of them forty days and speaking of the things pertaining to the kingdom of God; and, being assembled together with them, commanded them that they should not depart from Jerusalem, but wait for the promise of the Father," *i. e.*, the miraculous outpouring of the Holy Ghost. Having given His disciples some final instructions, He ascends into heaven from the mount called Olivet, about two miles east of Jerusalem. Hereupon followed His sitting at the right hand of God. Of this our text speaks.

We read: *"God set Him at His own right hand in the heavenly places."* Of whom does the apostle speak? Self-evidently of Christ, of Him who was raised from the dead and ascended into heaven; he therefore speaks of the exaltation of the man Christ. He now sits at the right hand of God. What does that mean? God is a spirit and has neither a right nor a left hand. It is a figurative expression, which bespeaks God's almighty power, wherefore it is called "the hand of His power," "the hand of His majesty." Here God *set* Christ. Christ is God, and the divine government belonged to Him from all eternity. According to His divine nature Christ cannot be said to be *set* at the right hand of God. The expression *set,* "God *set* Him," indicates that this was done according to Christ's human nature. The man Christ was exalted to an unceasing participation in the divine government. Also according to His human nature Christ is now forever the Ruler of the universe. Christ, who partook of the same flesh and blood that we have, our Brother, is seated upon the heavenly throne. What a mighty consolation for us: our Brother is the omniscient and almighty Ruler of the world! He knows all our needs and distresses, our trials and tribulations; we shall not want. For means it fails Him never who now sits at the right hand of God *"in the heavenly places,"* that is, in the sphere of glory and majesty.

Oh, if we would but always confidently believe this, there would be no need of fearing and trembling as so often is the case. For what does this mean: Christ sits at the right hand of God in the heavenly places? Most sublimely the apostle unfolds this thought. In virtue of this participation in the divine government, Christ is *"far above all principality, and power, and might, and dominion."* These names denote angels of light; these designations point to the superhuman power and might of the heavenly spirits. Observe how the text reads: "principality, *and* power, *and* might, *and* dominion." That serves to make the thought emphatic. The reader is invited to ponder each concept separately in order that he may become all the more impressed with the marvelous power of these holy angels. However powerful they may be, aye, though all their power and might be combined, yet there is one who possesses far greater power; for *"far above"* them all is He who sits at the right hand of God, Christ, and majestically rules over them. Christ, our Brother, is on the throne of majesty. "Why, then, are ye fearful, O ye of little faith?" This majestic Ruler is your Savior.

The circle of Christ's dominion widens: He is far above *"every name that is named, not only in this world, but also in that which is to come."* That says: Christ rules over all, whatever it may be, howsoever great and powerful it may be, wherever it may be found, here in time or in eternity. Let the heathen rage, and the kings of the earth set themselves, and the rulers take counsel together, against the Lord and against His Anointed, no power on earth can shake His throne. Whom should we fear?

And as if to round off his majestic thought and guard against all misconception as to what the rule of Christ, who is at the right hand of God, comprises, the apostle sweepingly asserts: *"And hath put"* in subjection, lastingly, permanently, *"all things under His feet,"* so that Christ exercises absolute sovereignty over *all things,* all creatures whatsoever, the very devils in hell not excepted. Heaven, earth, hell — all under His feet! What a mighty Ruler this man Christ is! And this God-man is our Savior. What a sweet consolation! This consolation is meant for us, the Christians. For the Christians Paul prays that the eyes of their understanding might be enlightened to know more and more what a glorious Savior this their Christ is. In the days of His flesh He said: "All power is given unto Me in heaven and in earth." He proved His assertion to be true. He rebuked the winds and the waves, and there was a great calm. He cast out evil spirits with His word. The leper is cleansed of his leprosy; the centurion's petition in behalf of his dying servant is answered. The young man at Nain is called to life; at His word, Lazarus comes from the grave. Rays of divine glory these — in the state of humiliation. Now He, the glorified Christ, is in the state of exaltation, and now He has come into the unceasing use, also according to His human nature, of the divine majesty, which was always His. And He is the same Savior to-day that He was then, with the same merciful heart. Will He not guard and protect us and His Church against all enemies? Hence,

> Commit whatever grieves thee
> At heart, and all thy ways,
> To Him who never leaves thee,
> On whom creation stays;
> Who freest courses maketh
> For clouds and air and wind,
> And who care ever taketh
> A path for thee to find.

2.

Great as is this consolation, it becomes still greater when we consider that Christ's sitting at the right hand of God also involves the fact that Christ is the Head of the Church.

The majestic thought of the apostle reaches its climax in the last clause: *"And gave Him to be the Head over all things to the Church, which is His body."* Him — this glorious majestic Ruler; Him — who is equal with God; Him — to whom all, heaven, earth, and hell, is made subject: *Him God gave as Head to the Church, i. e.,* the communion of saints, *which* — Church — *is His body.* He that is Head over all things as Ruler and Sovereign, Col. 2, 10, is at the same time the Head of the Church.

But the headship, the rule, over the Church is entirely different from His headship over all creatures. In the Kingdom of Power He rules by means of His omnipotence; in the Kingdom of Grace He rules with His gracious Word. In the true sense of the word, as head that possesses a body, Christ is Head of His Church only. Col. 1, 18. The unbelievers are not members of His spiritual body. "If any man hath not the Spirit of Christ, he is none of His." Rom. 8, 9. How great the dignity of the Church! Christ is the Head; the believers are the members of this spiritual body. As intimately as the head is connected with the body, so intimately is Christ connected with the Church. As the head governs the body, so this Head governs His body, the Church. The Church hears the Word of Truth, the Gospel of salvation. V. 13. That is Christ's voice; by it the body, the Church, is governed. Whatsoever the Head, Christ, wills, the body, the Church, executes. "One is your Master, even Christ." And again, whosoever persecutes the Christians persecutes Christ. Paul, on his way to Damascus to persecute the followers of Christ, heard the voice of the exalted Savior: "Saul, Saul, why persecutest thou *Me?*"

But another incomparable prerogative of the Church comes out in the last phrase: the Church is *"the fulness of Him that filleth all in all."* Christ, who fills all with His efficacious presence, also fills the Church with His gracious presence. From Him, the exalted Head, the plenitude of spiritual, heavenly blessings is communicated to His body, the Church. Out of His fulness, in the Word and Sacraments, we receive grace for grace.

What a glorious Savior we have! Ought we poor sinners not to thank God again and again for having made us partakers of the inheritance of the saints in light?

And now, let us again ponder the emphasis in the clause: "And *Him* He gave as Head over all things to the Church, which is His body." What does this unmistakably peculiar stress say? He that is so intimately connected with His Church, He that has given His heart's blood for it as the purchase-price, He is at the same time the Ruler of the universe, heaven, earth, and hell being made subject to Him, *and He will, therefore, rule and govern all things for the benefit of the Church.* True, "now we *see* not yet all things put under His feet," Heb. 2, 8; it is an article of faith. Though now we do not *see* all things put under His feet, yet the fact remains. The whole course of this world is shaped for the benefit of the Church. When a building is completed, the scaffold is taken away. When the last elect has been gathered into the fold, or, to change the figure, when the last stone has been placed in God's temple, the Church, Eph. 2, 19 ff., the scaffold of this world will be destroyed.

So the whole world still stands to-day for the benefit of the Church. When, at the time of Christ, the then known world was brought under one rule, that of the Roman Emperor, highroads were built connecting the entire vast domain, commerce was established along these routes, intercourse was made comparatively easy, one language, the Greek, was understood by all. These self-same means of communication the apostles used. Along these highroads they traveled, publishing the Gospel of the kingdom, thus building the Church. About the time of the Reformation the invention of printing books by movable type was made — for the benefit of the Church. The Bible could be easily and cheaply procured, and the Gospel could be widely spread. And the discovery of America! It, too, was for the benefit of the Church. Here, under the providence of God, the principle of separation of Church and State became an established fact — for the benefit of the Church. Even the persecution of the Church, in the last analysis, must serve for the benefit of the Church. Acts 17, 1 ff.

In yonder life, when the mists will have lifted and our vision will have become clear, we shall see that this whole universe, the governments, the rulers, "every name that is named," lay in the hollow of His hand who sitteth at the right hand of the Father, and that all and everything was made subservient to the building of His kingdom, the Church. Amen.

Christ's Second Coming.

ACTS 17, 31.

God hath appointed a day in the which He will judge the world in righteousness by that Man whom He hath ordained.

Scripture says: "It is appointed unto men once to die, but after this the Judgment." All people are agreed as to the truth of the first statement: "It is appointed unto men once to die." To deny it were folly. Daily observations corroborate this truth. But as to the second state-

ment: "after this the Judgment," worldly-minded people
scoff at it. We Christians know the second statement to
be as true as the first. Why? God says so. And all
mockery of unbelievers cannot change our faith. Mocking,
scoffing, does not require much brains, nor is it argument,
nor does it show originality. The family tree of the
mockers may easily be traced to Peter's time, aye, to
the days of Noah. Let us hear briefly what Peter has
to say of these enemies of the Gospel. Speaking of Christ's
second coming, he warns the Christians not to be misled,
saying: "Know this first, that there shall come in the
last days scoffers, walking after their own lusts and saying, Where is the promise of His coming? For since
the fathers fell asleep, all things continue as they were
from the beginning of the creation." These scoffers, says
Peter, are lustful, people doing the desires of the flesh,
people living in sin. To them the thought of Judgment
Day is awful; hence they try to strengthen themselves
and others in their evil way by jeering at the thought of
Christ's second coming. "You speak so much of the
promise of His coming," they say; "we see no signs of it.
Centuries have come and gone, but 'all things continue
as they were from the beginning of the creation.' The
world lasts on through all time; there was no change, and
there will be none."

In masterful fashion Peter puts the quietus on the
cavilings of the despicable fellows. "All things continue!" is that so? Wilfully, says he, they forget that
there was a Deluge in which the whole world, save eight
souls, was swept away. Do all things continue?! Again,
the scoffers speak of a creation. If there is a creation, as
they concede, there is a Creator, and then there is also
a Judge! The mockers are poor thinkers, indeed! The
antediluvian world lasted a long time. From Adam to
Noah, people had seen the sun rise and set daily. And

one day it rose, but the people did not see it set: the Deluge came and engulfed them all. Just so there will be a day on which the sun will rise, but before it has run its daily course, the Day of the Lord will have come, *i. e.,* the day the Lord has appointed to judge the world will be at hand. On this topic we shall speak this evening, *viz.,*

Christ's Second Coming.

Let us consider —

1. *The time of His coming;*
2. *The manner of His coming;*
3. *The purpose of His coming.*

1.

Paul stands on Mars Hill, famous Mars Hill, in Athens. Opposite him is the Acropolis, on which is the oldest heathen temple of Athens together with that masterpiece of architecture, the Parthenon, beside which is the patron goddess, Pallas Athena. In this highest seat of heathen culture, wisdom, and art, surrounded by adherents of the wisest of old-time philosophers, Paul preaches on "The Unknown God." We behold an audience entirely antagonistic to the Christian religion, an audience similar to one, if it were possible, gathered from all non-churchgoers of this city — the worldly wise, the learned; people puffed up about their knowledge, boasting of their enlightenment and culture. To such he discloses the vanity of their religion, teaches them the true God, and finally preaches the Gospel of repentance and faith, concluding with this saying: *"God hath appointed a day in the which He will judge the world in righteousness by that Man whom He hath ordained,"* Jesus Christ. See also Acts 10, 42.

Paul knew full well he was telling these Athenians a distasteful truth. He tells them of Christ's second coming to judge the world. Let us consider what he says: *God has appointed a day in which the Son of Man will come to judge.* Since He has *appointed* a day, it will surely come; it is a fixed day, decreed in His eternal counsels.

Not only has a certain definite *day* been decreed, but the very *hour* of Christ's coming to Judgment is fixed. Mark 13, 32. The precise time of His coming, however, is a profound secret to all mankind. Says our Lord: "Of that day and that hour knoweth no man, no, not the angels which are in heaven, neither the Son, but the Father." Mark 13, 32. Observe the climax: No man knows, no angel knows, not even the Son — in the state of His humiliation — knew. How futile and foolish, therefore, are the attempts of those wiseacres who, with pencil and pad in hand, endeavor to compute "that day and that hour"! Though we do not know the precise time, we do know that it is near at hand. Says Peter: "The end of all things is at hand." St. Paul admonishes the Philippians: "The Lord is at hand." St. John beseechingly warns the Christians: "Little children, it is the last hour."

Here again the scoffers believe to be able to score a point against Christ's religion: "Where is the promise of His coming?" say they. These words were written wellnigh two thousand years ago! We ask, Have Peter, Paul, and John erred? No. Why not? Let Peter answer. Speaking of the nearness of the Lord's coming, he adds: "Be not ignorant of this one thing, that one day is with the Lord as a thousand years and a thousand years as one day." These men spoke God's language; with God the end is at hand even though millenniums must still pass by. Nor is this a very remarkable fact if we reflect but a little. Ask a child, and it will tell you that a lifetime of fifty to eighty years is a long, long time; ask a man of eighty, and he will tell you that his lifetime was short and passed away like a fleeting shadow. Now, since time is such a very relative quantity even between man and man, how much reason have we to wonder that God's calendar as to time is vastly different from ours?

No, it remains unalterably true: God has appointed a day in which He will judge the world. In stentorian tones, in spite of all scoffing of the unbelievers, the watchmen on Zion's walls must cry out to the people: Do not allow yourselves to be lulled into security; the Day of the Lord will surely come. So He has said; His Word is truth.

Moreover, friends, is it not true that every man knows there will be a resurrection and a Judgment Day? Why was it—referring to that awful *Titanic* catastrophe—that almost every newspaper in the land reported with apparent satisfaction and relief that the last strains of music those poor victims heard were "Nearer, My God, to Thee"? Face to face with such an appalling disaster, the natural knowledge of God asserts itself; there is an undercurrent of feeling: Death does not end all; there is a life after death; man after death must face his Creator — God.

Though the exact time of Christ's coming to Judgment has, for wise purposes, not been revealed to us, still we know of its absolute certainty and its nearness.

2.

Now the question arises, *How* will Christ, the Judge of the quick and the dead, come? Our text does not explicitly tell us about the manner of Christ's coming to Judgment; it was not within the scope of the apostle's sermon to do so. But our text *suggests* the manner of His coming. We read: "God will judge the world . . . by that *Man* whom He hath ordained." "That Man" is Jesus Christ, and the expression designates Him according to His human nature. The Man Jesus will come visibly.

What is here thus hinted at other passages of Scriptures elaborate. When Jesus ascended into heaven forty days after His resurrection, the disciples, who saw Him ascend visibly, were told by the two angels standing by: "This same Jesus which is taken up from you into heaven shall so come in like manner as ye have seen Him go into heaven." All stress is here laid upon Christ's visible return. Who will return? The same Jesus who was born in Bethlehem, suffered, was crucified, died, and was buried, but who was raised again and was seen of them for forty days after His resurrection; the same Jesus who had just spoken to them and now had visibly departed from them, God's Son and Mary's son: He "shall so come," visibly, "in like manner as ye have seen Him go," visibly, gloriously, "into heaven." Acts 1, 11. He will not appear in poverty, like at His first coming, but "in great power and glory," as He Himself declared to His disciples (Matt. 16, 27): "The Son of Man shall come in the glory of His Father with His angels." And Paul says: "The Lord Himself shall descend from heaven with a shout, with the voice of the archangels and with the trump of God." 1 Thess. 4, 16. Then He "who is ordained of God to be the Judge of the quick and the dead" (Acts 10, 42) will be seen of all men; and "every tongue must confess," willingly or unwillingly, "that Jesus Christ is Lord, to the glory of God the Father." Phil. 2, 9—11.

On that last Great Day the Savior of mankind will come, not, however, as the Savior, — the time of grace will then have elapsed, — but as the Judge of the world. Of this purpose of Christ's second advent we shall now speak.

3.

Our text says: "*God hath appointed a day in the which He will judge the world in righteousness.*" The whole world, all nations, will be summoned before His tribunal.

"We must all appear before the judgment-seat of Christ."
2 Cor. 5, 10. No matter where or how we died: the earth,
the water, the crematories, all must give up their dead.
God will make that possible. The quick, the then living,
and all the dead, without exception, will be there.

In that great panorama unrolled before our eyes in
Matt. 25 we see the Son of Man coming in all His glory,
sitting upon the throne of His glory. Before Him are
gathered all nations, separated from each other as a shep-
herd divideth his sheep from the goats: the sheep, the
believers, on His right hand; the goats, the unbelievers,
on His left. Next the sentence is spoken: To those on
His right hand He says: "Come, ye blessed of My Father,
inherit the kingdom prepared for you from the foundation of the world." To those on the left, however, He will
say: "Depart from Me, ye cursed, into everlasting fire,
prepared for the devil and his angels."

Upon what will the sentence, "Come," or, "Depart,"
be based? The apostle says: He will judge *"in righteousness,"* i. e., His judgment will be an unerring judgment,
unerring justice will be meted out. It will be a public
judgment to vindicate His righteousness, proving that
He is no respecter of persons. The very damned themselves, conscious-smitten, must concede: "My damnation
is just."

How will that be effected? This righteous judgment
will be based upon the works of man. For, says St. Paul,
"we must all appear before the judgment-seat of Christ,
that every one may receive the things done in his body,
according to that he hath done, whether it be good or bad."
2 Cor. 5, 10. And St. Peter avers: God, "without respect
of persons, judgeth according to every man's work." 1 Pet.
1, 17. The good works of the believers will be produced in
evidence of their faith, the evil works of the unbelievers
in evidence of their unbelief. That is just as unerring

a rule as this: The good fruits bespeak a good tree, and
the bad fruits, or no fruits at all, bespeak a bad or a barren
tree. Thus all must appear in their true character. Thus
the judgment will be a righteous judgment. The outward
semblance of having been Christians will not save; hypoc-
risy will be no cloak here. The works are manifest proofs
whether one was for or against Christ.

But will also the evil works of the Christians be brought
to light? No. In that sublime account of Judgment
Day to which I have referred the Lord, when speaking
to those on His right, mentions only their good works in
proof of their being "the blessed of His Father." He says:
"I was an hungred, and ye gave Me meat; I was thirsty,
and ye gave Me drink. . . . Verily, I say unto you: Inas-
much as ye have done it unto one of the least of these My
brethren, ye have done it unto Me." Matt. 25, 35—40.
Not a single word is said about their evil deeds. Why?
Because the works, the good works, are to show that they
believed in Him, that they were His own, His disciples.
What has become of our evil deeds, our sins? Says
Jehovah: "I, even I, am He that blotteth out thy transgressions for Mine own sake and will not remember
thy sins."

Now, what is the rule according to which this righteous
judgment shall be rendered? "The Word that I have
spoken, the same shall judge him in the Last Day." John
12, 48. The same Word that we now hear, read, study,
this same Word shall judge man on that Day. And what,
in the last analysis, is that rule? "He that believeth and
is baptized shall be saved, but he that believeth not shall
be damned." Mark 16, 16. So here, in this life, the
eternal lot of man is sealed. There is no opportunity for
conversion after death.

Friends, I have not attempted to depict the unbounded
terror with which the hearts of unbelievers will be filled

when Judgment Day will appear; it is beyond human utterance. St. Peter says: "The Day of the Lord will come as a thief in the night, in the which the heavens shall pass away with a great noise, and the elements shall melt with fervent heat, the earth also and the works that are therein shall be burned up." But even as in the terrible havoc of the present* colossal World War, where the rattle of musketry, the din of battle, and the carnage of men is awful to the vanquished, while the same sounds are like liberty bells to the victors, so it will be on the Last Day. "When these things begin to come to pass, then look up and lift up your heads; for your redemption draweth nigh." Luke 21, 28. For the Christians the troubles of this life will then be past, and the joys of heaven will begin. "Beloved, now are we the sons of God, and it doth not yet appear what we shall be; but we know that, when He shall appear, we shall be like Him; for we shall see Him as He is." 1 John 3, 2. "Henceforth there is laid up for me a crown of righteousness, which the Lord, the righteous Judge, shall give me at that day, and not to me only, but unto all them also that love His appearing." 2 Tim. 4, 8.

But to the majority of mankind this day will come as a snare. "As the days of Noah were, so shall also the coming of the Son of Man be. For as in the days that were before the Flood they were eating and drinking, marrying and giving in marriage, until the day that Noah entered into the ark, and knew not until the Flood came and took them all away: so shall also the coming of the Son of Man be." Matt. 24, 37—39. In the words of a noted preacher: "Many will not believe it, but will make a mock of it. Thus many will be overwhelmed by sudden horror: some engaged in dark deeds of crime, some whirling the wanton waltz in revelry, some seeking to gain the

* This sermon was delivered during the days of the World War.

whole world and losing their souls, others living in security.
Darkness falls upon the earth, and all creation quakes,
shrieks, groans — the Lord has come, and Judgment falls
upon the unpardoned as a snare."

Oh, be ye ready; watch and pray! "Have you sinned?
Come to Jesus; there is forgiveness with Him. Do you
lack righteousness? Come to Jesus and claim His righteousness prepared for you. Now is the accepted time.
Now He invites you; now He offers you the garments of
salvation. Come, ye sinners, and wash yourselves in the
blood of Christ, and it will carry away your transgressions,
and in the Day of Judgment not a trace of sin will be
found." (Kuegele.)

> Delay not, delay not, O sinner, draw near,
> The waters of life are now flowing for thee.
> No price is demanded, the Savior is here;
> Redemption is purchased, salvation is free.

Amen.

The Rich Man in Hell.

LUKE 16, 23—25.

And in hell he lifted up his eyes, being in torments, and
seeth Abraham afar off and Lazarus in his bosom. And he
cried and said, Father Abraham, have mercy on me and send
Lazarus that he may dip the tip of his finger in water and cool
my tongue; for I am tormented in this flame. But Abraham
said, Son, remember that thou in thy lifetime receivedst thy
good things and likewise Lazarus evil things; but now he is
comforted, and thou art tormented.

Death! The Judgment! Eternity! What awful con-
cepts to contemplate! "It is appointed unto men once
to die, but after this the Judgment!" As there are but
two classes of people here on earth, the one for Christ,
the other against Him, believers and unbelievers, so at the
Judgment there will be but two classes, the one on the

right hand of Christ, to whom He says, "Come!" and the other on the left, who must hear the awful words, "Depart from Me!" Those at His right are "they that have done good," the Christians; those on His left are "they that have done evil," the non-Christians; the former have been called forth out of their graves "to the resurrection of life," the latter "to the resurrection of damnation." John 5, 28. 29.

Now, as there are but two classes of men, so there are but two abodes for men after death: heaven and hell. But as surely as there is a heaven for believers, so surely is there a hell for unbelievers.

Is it not a sad commentary on our times that even so self-evident a truth of Scriptures as this must be stressed? We are living in the last sad times. Formerly, unbelievers who scoffed at everything religious also scoffed at the idea of there being a hell; but they scoffed alone. Nowadays, however, they have found a mouthpiece for their unbelief, a man who poses* as a Christian preacher, a certain Russell, whose so-called sermons are widely disseminated by the secular press, paid for, of course, by his adherents. Since his unscriptural effusions have been scattered far and wide, it becomes necessary to raise the voice of warning against them. He maintains, among other things, that, while there is a heaven, there is no hell. Unbelievers will, after death, get another chance to accept the Gospel-message, and if then they still reject Christ as their Savior, they will be annihilated. To consign human beings to hell, says he, is contrary to God's mercy and love. Every Christian can easily judge for himself whether this spirit is from God or not. But the devil, whose tool Russell is, shrinks back at nothing. These flat denials of clear testimonies of Scripture are made in public print and before large audiences.

---

* Russell was still living when this sermon was delivered.

Christ said, in sending out His disciples: "Fear not them which kill the body, but are not able to kill the soul; but rather fear Him which is able to destroy both soul and body in hell." So there is a hell. And in unfolding that great panorama of the Last Day, Christ says: "Depart from Me, ye cursed, into everlasting fire, prepared for the devil and his angels." So there is a hell.

But why multiply instances? Our text also loudly proclaims the fact that there is a hell. It is a graphic portraiture that we have here of that awful place of torments. In drawing the picture, Christ draws aside the veil hanging between time and eternity and affords us a glimpse of yonder world. Three persons are depicted. The rich man is in the foreground — in hell; Lazarus and Abraham in heaven serve as a foil in the painting to set off in bold relief the misery of the damned rich man. The rich man's lot will be the fate of all unbelievers. Let us consider — an appalling subject indeed —

The Rich Man in Hell.

1. The torment he there endures;
2. The cause of his damnation.

1.

"And in hell he lifted up his eyes, being in torments, and seeth Abraham afar off and Lazarus in his bosom. And he cried and said, Father Abraham, have mercy on me and send Lazarus that he may dip the tip of his finger in water and cool my tongue; for I am tormented in this flame." The text is self-explanatory. Hell is a place of torment, of excruciating pain. This agony is caused by the flame of hell-fire. Now, we must not imagine the fire of hell to be anything like our mundane fire, which consumes everything that is cast into it. Hell-fire is a fire adapted to the circumstances there existing; it is a fire more horrible than any human mind can begin to imagine.

The fire of hell will not consume those assigned to it, but will torment them forever and ever. In the language of Revelation: "The smoke of their torments ascendeth up forever and ever." As our earthly fire causes its victims to writhe and shriek with the intensity of their suffering, — this is the point of resemblance, — so hell-fire will cause the most horrible agony, insomuch that, as Christ says elsewhere, "there will be weeping and gnashing of teeth."

How great the suffering will be we may glean from the pitiful petition of the rich man. "He cried and said, Father Abraham, have mercy on me and send Lazarus that he may dip the tip of his finger in water and cool my tongue." He begs for a single drop of water to cool his parched tongue, and even this is denied him. Even this alleviation of pain for the hundredth part of a minute he would look upon as being mercy shown him. But no; hell is a place where mercy is no longer granted. The time of mercy has ceased, that of punishment, incessant punishment, has begun. And this inexpressible torment is to last forever. According to our Lord's own statements this fire "never shall be quenched"; it is "an everlasting fire," "an everlasting destruction," "an everlasting punishment." Hell is a place where the inmates shall have "no rest day or night."

Not only in their bodies shall they be so tormented, but also in their souls. *"Son, remember that thou in thy lifetime receivedst thy good things."* The memory of these "good things," once so highly cherished, but now cursed as follies, will be forever with them, and they will unceasingly deplore the fact that for these frivolities they bartered eternal bliss. They will remember the misspent Sundays, when, instead of hearing "Moses and the prophets" expounded, they followed their lustful inclinations; they will remember the solemn admonitions not heeded, the faithful sermons they disregarded. Their conscience will accuse them continually, saying: We might have escaped this terrible doom; mercy was extended to us, but we rejected it. We were warned and entreated. The Savior stretched forth His hands also toward us; we spurned them. And now? These are the wages of sin. Now we experience the awful reality of the words spoken by Him whom we despised. "Their worm," the accusations of an evil conscience, "shall not die, neither shall their fire be quenched." Do you know what it means to have an evil conscience? Have you not read of people who, after having committed a foul crime, found rest neither night nor day until they gave themselves up to justice? What untold agonies, then, will it inflict on the damned in hell "where their worm dieth not"!

Still another thing to aggravate the misery in hell will be the company of the damned. The rich man in hell called to Abraham in heaven: *"I pray thee therefore, Father, that thou wouldst send him* [Lazarus] *to my father's house; for I have five brethren; that he may testify unto them, lest they also come into this place of torment."* Why this prayer? Out of pity to his brothers? No; the damned know of no pity. The rich man feared the coming of his brothers to this place because they would forever upbraid him as being the cause of their damnation. "You," they would say, "have scoffed at Moses and the prophets and caused us to scoff. Oftentimes, by your jeers and jibes, you prevented us from hearing their voice. You were the leader in wickedness. You made light of the Word of God and seduced us to do the same." By such or similar accusations his misery would be but enhanced, hence the petition: Send Lazarus to them to warn them.

Though the punishment of all will be a comfortless, rayless, hopeless hell, still the degrees of torment will differ according to different degrees of guilt. In Luke 12 the Lord illustrates this truth. He speaks of two servants.

The one knew his lord's will, the other did not. Both were beaten, the latter with few stripes, the former, though knowing his master's will, yet not doing according to it, with many stripes. The reason adduced is: "For unto whomsoever much is given, of him shall be much required." The greater the grace, the greater the damnation. What a warning to us Lutherans, to whom the Lord has committed so much — His Word pure and undefiled! What terrible punishments do they call down upon themselves, who, knowing the will of God, still run with the world to the same excess of riot!

May God in His mercy grant that we be preserved from entering this place of awful torments! To this end let us inquire what brought the rich man there.

2.

The rich man was *"clothed in purple and fine linen."* Were these things the cause of his damnation? No. Riches, fine garments, an honorable station in life, are not causes of damnation. Solomon, David, Esther, to mention but a few worthies of the Old Testament, were rich, exalted, arrayed in fine vestments. Wealth in itself is a blessing, not a curse.

What was wrong with the rich man? He *"fared sumptuously every day."* This manifests the sentiment of his heart. His heart was centered on the things of this world; he lived only for the "good things" of this world; he was carnally minded; the belly was his god; this earth, his heaven. Riches, in themselves a blessing, had proved a snare to his feet. How much good could the rich man have done to Lazarus! How much suffering might he have alleviated! But no, there is no thought for others.

Why this? Because he was a godless person. Had he been a Christian, he would have considered himself a steward of God and used his wealth accordingly. But

the rich man was a godless man. He had cared nothing
for Moses and the prophets, the Word of God. Their words
had been a matter of complete indifference to him. *Unbelief* was the cause of his damnation.

He has five brothers. He asks Abraham to send Lazarus
to warn them. In hell the rich man turns spiritualist.
Spiritualism is a doctrine of devils. What does Abraham
say to the request made? *"They have Moses and the
prophets; let them hear them."* The rich man is not
satisfied. He does not believe in the saving power of God's
Word. *"Nay, Father Abraham,"* says he, *"but if one went
unto them from the dead, they will repent."* Unbelievers
are very wise in their own conceit. God's way to save mankind does not appeal to them; they have better plans;
they are wiser than God. Unbelievers are spiritually dead
and know not the power of God; they are religiously
insane.

Abraham makes answer: *"If they hear not Moses and
the prophets, neither will they be persuaded though one
rose from the dead."* "Moses and the prophets" is the
court of last resort. "The Word that I have spoken, the
same shall judge him on the last day," says the Lord. We
are to be saved by a believing hearing of the Word, not
by ghosts.

Why was the rich man damned? Because he rejected
Moses and the prophets, the mouthpieces of God. Unbelief
damns. The rich man was an unbeliever: his whole life
proves that he was a godless person.

The only means of effectually converting the sinner is
the living Word of God. If Moses and the prophets are
despised, the only alternative is hell. "Search the Scriptures," says the Lord, "for in them ye think ye have eternal
life; and they are they which testify of Me." If Moses
and the prophets, the Scriptures, do not save man, nothing
in heaven and on earth can save him. The Word of God

is the only power that can turn people "from idols to the living God," "from the power of Satan unto God." Moses and the prophets, the Scripture, the Gospel, is "the power of God unto salvation to every one that believeth," the only God-appointed means "to make wise unto salvation." Reject it, and God rejects you. Unbelief damns.

How full the world is to-day of men harboring the same sentiments as those of the rich man! Like the rich man they say: There is no resurrection, no Judgment, no hell; and with the rich man they will forever piteously cry for a drop of water to cool their blasphemous tongue. With the rich man they believe in new revelations from the other world, and with him they shall forever hear dinning in their ears: "They have Moses and the prophets; let them hear them." With the rich man they believe that messages from hell would be more effective than messages from heaven to turn the world to God, and with him they will be condemned to that place prepared for the devil and his angels. Unbelief damns.

Is so-called Christian Science right? The rich man received the answer: "They have Moses and the prophets." Is Spiritualism right? The rich man, on demanding that Lazarus be sent to testify to his five brothers, was told: "They have Moses and the prophets; let them hear them." Is there a purgatory, as the Catholics teach? "The rich man died and was buried." And then what? "In hell he lifted up his eyes." Is there a state of second probation after death, where man is given another chance to accept the Gospel-message he here despised? The rich man is told: The only means that can save your five brothers from this place of torment is Moses and the prophets.

O friends, how many, by false doctrines, would rob us of our Bible! Satan is using his old device to this day with good effect: "Yea, hath God said?" Therefore, "Hold that fast which thou hast!" What Moses and the prophets say must be the only subject the Christian preacher enlarges on in the pulpit. What say Moses and the prophets? this is the demand the pew must make of the preacher.

But let us not hear the Word of God merely externally. Let us, by the grace of God, accept its teachings with a believing heart, and let us, above all, embrace the glorious Gospel-truth that "Christ Jesus came into the world to save sinners," to save them from sin, the devil, and the eternal torments of hell. "Neither is there salvation in any other; for there is none other name under heaven given among men whereby we must be saved." So say Moses and the prophets, the evangelists and the apostles. And, believing in Christ, let us walk as His disciples to please God. Let us shun sin, from which we have been redeemed. If God has granted us riches, let us use them as good stewards of God for poor Lazarus and the spread of the kingdom of God.

And when death comes, we shall fall asleep in Jesus, and as truly as "we believe that Jesus died and rose again, even so them also which sleep in Jesus will God bring with Him" to rise to everlasting life, and with Lazarus be forever comforted in Abraham's bosom.

God grant unto us all such a blessed end for Jesus' sake! Amen.

The Blessedness of the Believers.

1 JOHN 3, 1. 2.

Behold, what manner of love the Father hath bestowed upon us, that we should be called the sons of God! Therefore the world knoweth us not, because it knew Him not. Beloved, now are we the sons of God, and it doth not yet appear what we shall be; but we know that, when He shall appear, we shall be like Him; for we shall see Him as He is.

Oh, for the sad fall of our first parents! How changed became the relation of man towards God and things divine thereby! Man, by nature, is no longer a child of God, but a "child of wrath," "dead in trespasses and sins."

Speaking to the Ephesians, St. Paul draws this gloomy picture of their spiritual condition before their conversion: "Wherefore remember that ye, being in time past Gentiles in the flesh, ... that at that time ye were without Christ, ... having no hope, and without God in the world." Without Christ! Without hope! Without God! Terrible, indeed, beyond the power of expression of human speech, is the spiritual condition of natural man.

And this is a pen-picture of all unchristians to this day. It matters not who they may be, what exalted station in life they may occupy or may have occupied: heroes of history, men of deep learning, great poets, painters, statesmen, men of moral integrity in the eyes of the world, — if unconverted, they are without Christ, without hope, without God, children of wrath!

And their end — despite all their refinement, culture, learning, and morality — their end, if this wrath is not taken away — damnation, the place "where their worm dieth not and their fire shall not be quenched."

Now, it is not the will of the Father that any should perish, but that all should come to the knowledge of the truth. Hence His ministers cry, "Be ye reconciled to God."

And thanks be to God for His great love wherewith He loved us! We, too, once were dead in trespasses and sins; but "He hath quickened us together with Christ, and hath raised us up together, and made us sit together in heavenly places in Christ Jesus." With St. Peter we can triumphantly exclaim: "Blessed be the God and Father of our Lord Jesus Christ, which, according to His abundant

mercy, hath begotten us again unto a lively hope by the
resurrection of Jesus Christ from the dead, to an inheritance incorruptible, and undefiled, and that fadeth not
away, reserved in heaven."

Deplorable as is the condition of the unbelievers, so
blessed is the condition of the believers. Of this great
bliss we shall speak to-day.

The Blessedness of the Believers,

1. Here in time,   *2. Yonder in eternity.*

1.

"Behold, what manner of love the Father hath bestowed
upon us, that we should be called the sons," the children,
"of God!"

What a jubilant strain this is! How the very reading
of the text thrills the soul and lifts it upward and onward!
One hesitates to explain the text, lest its beauty and force
be lost upon the heart. Its very simplicity and grandeur
grips the heart and speaks volumes of the Father's love.

Hear it again: "Behold, what manner of love the
Father hath bestowed upon us, that we should be called the
sons of God!" *We* — the sons of God! Why, then we
belong to God's family; God is our Father; heaven is
our home; eternal life is our certain inheritance.

How incomprehensible this love of the Father! For
what a gulf is there between us sinful beings and the holy
God that such a relation as children and Father could ever
come to pass! To be the son of an exalted king, that is
high honor; but a higher honor is here! If a prince adopts
a waif from the street and for his tatters and rags clothes
him in princely costume, that is a manifestation of great
love; but a greater love is here! When David spares the
life of his enemy Saul, that bespeaks great love; but
a greater love is here!

"Behold, what manner of love the Father hath bestowed

upon us, that we should be called the sons of God!" Who
are we that the Father should bestow such love upon us?
By nature we are children of wrath. "We are all as an
unclean thing, and all our righteousnesses are as filthy
rags." Spiritually we are like the Prodigal Son, who
wasted his inheritance by riotous living. We are sinners
and as such should die eternally; aye, by nature we are
enemies of God.

But behold, what love the Father bestowed upon us:
He calls us His sons, His children! How did this come
about? Not did we seek Him; He sought us and bestowed
this title upon us. The same John writes in the next
chapter: "God is Love. In this was manifested the love
of God toward us, because that God sent His only-begotten
Son into the world that we might live through Him.
Herein is love, not that we loved God, but that He loved
us, and sent His Son to be the propitiation for our sins."
Sin separated us from God. God is just. Sin must be
atoned for. We could not do it. God did it for us. His
Son made propitiation for our sins. Thus sin was atoned
for; now eternal life is in store for sinners.

But we were dead in sin; we cared not for this manifestation of love. So God's love went farther. His Son
not only sacrificed Himself for us, but also taught the way
to the Father. He pleaded: "Come unto Me, all ye that
labor and are heavy laden, and I will give you rest." He
sought that which was lost. And His seeking love found us.
We recognized our lost condition and sought refuge in
His bosom. Thus we became His own; thus we became
children of God. For we "are all the *children of God*
by faith in Christ Jesus."

What wonderful condescending love of the Father that
we, who are by nature heirs of sin and guilt, children of
corruption and disobedience, should be made the sons of
God! A more splendid crown of glory no king has ever

worn. We are monuments of God's love. Small wonder that John so exultingly cries out: "What manner of love the Father hath bestowed upon us!" And, as if to point out the greatness of this bliss, lest it be overlooked, he prefixes it with the significant exclamation, "Behold!"

Great cause, truly, we Christians have to rejoice at all times, since we are the sons of God. But the trouble with us is that we are not always conscious of our dignity; we still have the flesh, which clouds our spiritual vision. For this very reason we are told in the Scripture: Ye Christians *are* the sons of God — rejoice!

The world, of course, knows nothing of this great bliss of the Christians. The world believes the Christians to be of all men most miserable. The world believes the Christians to be an object of pity and ridicule, because the world, men in their unregenerate condition, lack the spiritual eye. The deaf cannot enjoy the wonderful music of a Mozart, a Beethoven, a Schumann; the blind cannot see the wonderful works of creation and art; the spiritually deaf and blind cannot comprehend the blessedness of "the children of God." Why not? "They know not God." Says St. John: "For this cause the world knoweth us not, because it knew Him not."

But what of it, if the world does not know and acknowledge our honor, dignity, and bliss as children of God? The king that has donned the beggar's garb is not recognized by his subjects. We are princes traveling *incognito* through this world. Like Master, like subject. Our Savior, while on earth, was the Father's true, eternally begotten Son — the world knew Him not; we are sons by adoption, our dignity is hidden — small wonder the world knows us not.

But what of it? The fact remains: "Beloved, now *are* we the sons of God." But is it not true that we must suffer the calamities of earth and time as well as others? Is it not true that the Christians oftentimes must suffer more than others? It is. But remember, we are still in the land of strangers. Here the rule is: "We must through much tribulation enter into the kingdom of God." Was there ever any one who suffered more for Christ's sake than Paul? He was a child of God. Was there any one who suffered greater calamities than Job? Amidst all his sufferings he was a child of God. And Lazarus, was he not a child of God? So, "brethren, think it not strange concerning the fiery trial which is to try you, as though some strange thing happened unto you."

The blessedness of this sonship manifests itself in an entirely different way. If Satan would terrify the Christian on account of his sins, saying: "Here is the Law, 'Thou shalt!' 'The soul that sinneth, it shall die,'" the child of God answers: "As long as I was without Christ, you could thus accuse me, but since God is my Father through Christ, 'who is he that condemneth? It is Christ that died, yea, rather, that is risen again; who is even at the right hand of God; who also maketh intercession for us.'" When cross and tribulation enters his threshold, and the fiery darts of the Evil One assail him, "You a child of God and suffer such things!" he makes answer: "Who shall separate us from the love of Christ? Shall tribulation, or distress, or persecution, or famine, or nakedness, or peril, or sword? Nay, in all these things we are more than conquerors through Him that loved us." And when death knocks at his door, the child of God says, "I am persuaded that neither death, nor life, nor angels, nor principalities, nor powers, nor things present, nor things to come, nor height, nor depth, nor any other creature, shall be able to separate us from the love of God, which is in Christ Jesus, our Lord." "I have a desire to depart and to be with Christ."

Such is, in faint outline, the blessedness of the believers

here in time. Here our sonship is hidden; "it is not yet made manifest what we shall be." That manifestation lies beyond the grave, in yonder life. Of this blessedness we shall now speak.

2.

"Beloved, now are we the sons of God, and it doth not yet appear what we shall be." Our sonship is a reality. Great is our present blessed condition; but far greater things are in store for us. This sonship, hidden now, will one day be revealed. "It doth not yet appear what we shall be"; but it will become manifest in the future. The robe of righteousness with which we are now clothed is not patent to the eye; the crown of glory that adorns our head is as yet invisible, and what great blessedness awaits us even we Christians cannot apprehend.

But some things we do know because they are revealed in Scriptures, and among these is: *"We know that we shall be like Him."* "We know"; it is not fiction, fancy, imagination; we know — here is positive knowledge, more reliable than the evidence of the senses, surer knowledge than that gained, say, by a mathematical demonstration. We know because God tells us so. What do we know? One day "He," Christ, "shall appear" in great glory with all His holy angels and with the trump of God.

Then all that are in the graves shall come forth; we Christians, the sons of God, will meet the Lord in the air. Our vile bodies will be changed like unto the glorious body of Christ; we shall possess a spiritual, glorified body, as Paul says to the Philippians. The image of God, lost through the Fall, and renewed according to the beginning in this life, in yonder life will be fully restored. *"We shall be like Him."* What great blessedness this! We do not become gods; we remain "children of God," but children, sons, of God glorified. This we know to be true. Why? Because *"we shall see Him as He is."* With the eyes of our glorified body we shall see Him, Jesus, Lord, Jehovah, *"as He is."* With Job we triumphantly exclaim: "Though after my skin worms destroy this body, yet in my flesh shall I see God: whom I shall see for myself, and mine eyes shall behold, and not another." All the glory of yonder life that is to be ours, St. John compresses into this one clause: "We shall see Him *as He is."* That there will be no more crying, or pain, or such like is here presupposed as self-evident. That at His right hand there will be pleasures forevermore, likewise. This saying: *"We shall see Him as He is,"* goes deeper. We shall see God as to His essence and His properties. We shall know and see, for example, the mystery of the Trinity in unity, the mystery of the incarnation of Christ, and other deep doctrines of the Bible that we here believed.

Then, too, His ways, so often past finding out here below, will be manifest to us. Questions such as these often occur to us: Why must I go through this or that suffering? Why did this calamity befall me? But there is no answer. Then, however, we shall know and see what we here believed, "that all things work together for good to them that love God"; for *"we shall see Him as He is."* Then we shall see that it was His loving-kindness that led us all the days of our life, albeit through devious paths, to reach the eternal goal. "Now," as the Apostle says, 1 Cor. 13, "we see through a glass, darkly, but then face to face. Now I know in part, but then shall I know even as also I am known."

Here we know much of the beauty, the grandeur, the glory of Paradise, but when we shall come to a realization of the joys of yonder life, we shall see that our knowledge of heavenly things gained by Scripture was true, but that, great though it was, it is far surpassed by the realization of the things themselves.

To this heavenly bliss we may apply the words of

St. Paul, that "eye hath not seen, nor ear heard, neither have entered into the heart of man, the things which God hath prepared for them that love Him."

Truly, to see our Savior face to face, to see God "as He is," this is blessedness unspeakable. And all this bliss is ours now already by faith in Christ Jesus. No wonder St. John exultingly exclaims: "Behold, what manner of love the Father hath bestowed upon us, that we should be called the sons of God! Therefore the world knoweth us not, because it knew Him not. Beloved, now are we the sons of God, and it doth not yet appear what we shall be; but we know that, when He shall appear, we shall be like Him; for we shall see Him as He is."

God keep us steadfast in the faith unto our end for Christ's sake! Amen.

Job's Triumphant Song of Faith in View of Death.

JOB 19, 25—27.

I know that my Redeemer liveth, and that He shall stand at the latter day upon the earth; and though after my skin worms destroy this body, yet in my flesh shall I see God, whom I shall see for myself, and mine eyes shall behold, and not another.

The confession of the Christian Church, "I believe in the resurrection of the body and the life everlasting," is the doctrine of the Old Testament as well as that of the New. One of the most brilliant of the numerous gems of the Old Testament giving testimony to this fact we shall consider to-day. How clearly it speaks of the Redeemer's work, of the resurrection of the body, and of the life everlasting! If we did not know its author, we might presume it to be culled from a book of one of the New Testament writers. And still Job lived about 1500 years before Christ.

Let us briefly recall to our minds the dark background of the text by means of the context, and the rich consolation of Job's utterance will be all the more discernible.

Job is sorely afflicted; humanly speaking, a cure of his disease is out of the question; he is soon to die. His servants, his friends, his kinsfolk, his brothers, are estranged from him; even his own wife has turned against him, taunting him for his faith in God. His "counselors" have no sympathy for him. He is smitten of God for his wickedness — this they give him to understand. Yea, God Himself seems to be his enemy.

And out of the depth of this great misery rises this joyful hymn of faith and triumph! Job looks beyond grave and decay and death, and there beholds the Redeemer and His work, beholds the day of resurrection of the body and of eternal bliss. Let us consider

Job's Triumphant Song of Faith in View of Death.

1. I know that my Redeemer lives.

2. At the latter day He will raise my body from the grave.

3. I shall see God.

1.

"*I know that my Redeemer liveth,*" thus Job triumphantly exclaimed in firm faith, though encompassed by great earthly misery. In view of grim death, which makes the unbeliever quake and shake with fear and dread, we hear from the lips of the believing Job this song of victory. "*I know,*" I am firmly convinced of the thing whereof I speak; it is not a vague idea, an uncertain hope, but an unwavering trust, founded upon the solid rock of faith anchored in the Word of God. And what is it that Job so solemnly avers to know? "I know that *my Redeemer*

liveth." Who is this Redeemer of whom Job speaks? None
other than He whom we Christian people of the New Testament adore as such — Jesus Christ. Job says this Redeemer will raise him from the dead. This is a work of
our Lord Jesus, who says to Martha: "I am the Resurrection and the Life." Job furthermore asserts that this
Redeemer will lead him to a beatific vision of God. This,
too, is a work of the Savior. The Redeemer of whom Job
speaks is the promised Messiah, who was to redeem Israel
from sin, and to whom the believing Israelites looked
forward as their Savior, just as we Christians of the New
Testament era look backward to the work of redemption
accomplished nineteen hundred years ago.

When Job exultingly cries out, "I know that my
Redeemer *liveth,"* he views in firm faith the coming
Redeemer's work as already completed; and so it was in
the sight of God. Satan, sin, death, Job knows, will assail
Christ; a mighty warfare is to be waged between the
Woman's Seed and the devil. In this terrible struggle
waged to rescue mankind from the clutches of Satan, the
Redeemer's heel will be bruised: Christ must die for the
sins of the world, but death cannot retain Him, for He
is the Prince of Life. "Through death He destroyed him
that had the power of death, that is, the devil." The
redemption-money is paid. Satan is vanquished. The cry
on the cross, "It is finished!" is true. In proof thereof
the mighty Victor rises from the grave on the third day —
the Redeemer lives, and will forever live. Of this Redeemer,
who has tasted death for all, Job confidently asserts: He
is *my* Redeemer. He has redeemed *me* from the power of
the devil, hell, and death. By faith he appropriates the
merits of the Savior unto himself, and thus overcomes
the terrors of death.

Job's faith is our faith, his hymn of triumph, too, is
ours. We need a Redeemer. "There is no difference, for

all have sinned and come short of the glory of God." Our
sins separate between us and God. The wages of sin is
death. The world is lost in sin. Where is there a way
of escape? There is none, none that man can devise.
But what man cannot do God did. "God sent forth His
Son, made of a woman, made under the Law, to redeem
them that were under the Law." Now there is redemption
in Christ Jesus. "He that believeth in Me," these are the
Savior's words, "though he were dead, yet shall he live;
and whosoever liveth and believeth in Me shall never die."
Christ, our Redeemer, died for us and rose again. And
He promises His disciples: "Because I live, ye shall live
also." In this Messiah, this Jesus, Job put his trust, and
so do we.

Blessed are we. We are free from debt, punishment,
and the dominion of sin; we are happy children of God.
And we have a *living* Savior, who, according to His promise,
is with us all the days of our life in His Word and Sacraments. Again and again, through His Gospel, He assures
us of the forgiveness of sins. He is with us to fight for
and with us against the devil, who endeavors to ensnare us
again in his meshes. He proves Himself to be our living
Redeemer. The victory is ours. In view of death we, too,
may triumphantly sing:

> Jesus, my Redeemer, lives!
> I, too, unto life must waken;
> Endless joy my Savior gives;
> Shall my courage, then, be shaken?
> Shall I fear? Or could the Head
> Rise and leave His members dead?

Most assuredly not, for *at the latter day He will raise my
body from the grave.*

2.

Our text reads: *"He shall stand at the latter day upon
the earth; and though after my skin worms destroy this
body, yet in my flesh shall I see God."*

The whole earth — this is the sublime conception of the text — is one vast sepulcher, in which the dead rest. Job views himself as being dead and bedded in this grave, the earth. But on this earth, on this dust of his, the Redeemer is pictured as *standing* in all His glory, power, and majesty. He is *standing*, ready to manifest His power at the latter day. Then He will indeed prove Himself to be Job's Redeemer.

What will He do on this "latter day," "the day of the Lord," on Judgment Day? In the words of the text: "And though after my skin worms destroy this body, yet in my flesh shall I see God." Job says: My skin will be destroyed, my body will turn to dust and ashes in the grave, but there will be a glorious resurrection day, when my body will again be clothed with the selfsame skin I now possess. Job heaps words upon words to make this *knowledge* of his, his belief, clear. — *"And mine eyes shall behold"*; the eyes he now possesses shall be restored to him, and with these identical eyes he will behold God. And as if to make the meaning still plainer, he adds: "and not another," which says emphatically: I shall then be the same person with the same eyes and the same body that I now possess. I shall come forth from the grave with body and soul reunited, and enter eternal bliss. This I *know*, of this I am absolutely sure, because "my Redeemer liveth." With the Christians of the New Testament, Job triumphantly confesses: "I believe in the resurrection of the body."

> I am only flesh and blood,
> And on this corruption seizeth;
> But I know my Lord and God
> From the grave my body raiseth.

How clear is this knowledge of Job as to the resurrection of the body! When reading the words of our text, are we not at once reminded of St. Paul's dictum to the Philippians: "Our conversation," our citizenship, "is in heaven"? Here we are but "sojourners and pilgrims," and "we look for the Savior, the Lord Jesus Christ." What will happen at His second coming? "He shall change our vile body that it may be fashioned like unto His glorious body." Essentially this coincides with what Job says, and adds a beautiful truth. This "vile," *i. e.,* sinful, frail, corruptible body will be transformed into a glorious body. The body will be the same we had here, but it will be glorified like unto Christ's glorious body. When the Lord rose from the dead, He did not have a new body, but the one taken from the essence of the Virgin Mary. His disciples knew Him: they saw the selfsame Master; they heard the selfsame voice. To assure them that He was not a spirit, He showed them His wounds. "A spirit hath not flesh and bones, as ye see Me have," He said to them. Luke 24, 39. When they still doubted, He ate and drank with them. But His body had new qualities, new endowments. He did not come and go now, after the resurrection, as He had been wont to do, after the manner of men. He appeared to the disciples of Emmaus and — vanished. Suddenly He is amongst His disciples — they knew not whence He came; just as suddenly He departs, they knew not whither. Barred doors are no hindrance to Him. He was no longer limited by time or space. Christ's glorified body was a *spiritual* body. Such ours will be.

What a glorious thing this is that we have contemplated! Who can understand it? Job is not troubled about this question. He knows it to be a fact: *"In my flesh shall I see God."* Does the question, How can this be? trouble you? Paul has answered it. He says: Let the Lord attend to that. He will and can do it, "according to the working whereby He is able even to subdue all things unto Himself."

We Christians know that we, too, must die, but we also

know that death cannot hold us. Our Redeemer Himself
assures us: "This is the will of Him that sent Me, that
every one which seeth the Son, and believeth on Him, may
have everlasting life; and I will raise him up at the
last day."

So, then, my beloved Christian friend, dry your tears
at the grave of your beloved ones; look beyond death
and decay to the joyful Resurrection Day. We need not
sorrow as others who have no hope. And as we contemplate our own death, let us look steadfastly to Jesus, the
Conqueror of death, and as certainly as He lives, so certain
it is that we, too, shall live.

> Nay, too closely am I bound
> Unto Him by hope forever;
> Faith's strong hand the Rock hath found,
> Grasped it, and will leave it never;
> Not the ban of death can part
> From its Lord the trusting heart.

3.

And after the resurrection, what? *"I shall see God."*
This is the purpose for which Job shall be raised — to see
God. In these few words, "I shall see God," Job condenses
all the happiness of eternal life awaiting him. In this
beatific vision of God, in this seeing of his Redeemer,
who ransomed him with His blood, eternal bliss chiefly
consists.

What a contrast! Job in his suffering state now; in
his blissful state then! Here despised and mocked by his
friends, aye, even by his own wife, in dire distress, his body
wasted by sickness; there sound in body, in a glorified
state, at the right hand of God, where there are pleasures
forevermore; honored by God, in the company of all the
holy angels, saints, martyrs, Christians from all climes and
times. What a sublime hope in view of death! And a hope
that maketh not ashamed; for it is founded on the eternal

truth of God. This happy prospect causes Job to dwell upon and unfold this blessed truth. He says: I shall *see* God, my eyes shall *behold* Him and not another. This I know to be an absolute fact because "my Redeemer liveth."

What Job here triumphantly proclaims as his unshakable faith, St. John in the New Testament has put in the beautiful words: "Beloved, now are we the sons of God, and it doth not yet appear what we shall be; but we know that, when He shall appear, we shall be like Him; for we shall see Him as He is." And St. Paul, consoling the Christians in their multitudinous afflictions, writes to the Romans: "I reckon that the sufferings of this present time are not worthy to be compared with the glory which shall be revealed in us."

How blessed we Christians are by God's grace! We must die, but our death is only a sleep, upon which follows an awakening. When the Lord, our living Redeemer, shall appear on the Last Day in company with the host of angels, in the clouds of heaven, when His almighty voice shall pierce the graves, and the dead in Christ shall rise to eternal life, "when this corruptible shall have put on incorruption, and this mortal shall have put on immortality, then shall be brought to pass the saying that is written, Death is swallowed up in victory." Then we shall triumphantly shout: "O death, where is thy sting? O grave, where is thy victory? But thanks be to God, which giveth us the victory through our Lord Jesus Christ." Aye, then we shall experience what we here with Job believe and confess in view of all our spiritual enemies, in view of death: "I know that my Redeemer liveth, and that He shall stand at the latter day upon the earth; and though after my skin worms destroy this body, yet in my flesh shall I see God, whom I shall see for myself, and mine eyes shall behold, and not another." Amen.

Christ's Instruction on Prayer.

JOHN 16, 23. 24.

Verily, verily, I say unto you, Whatsoever ye shall ask the Father in My name, He will give it you. — Ask, and ye shall receive.

"Rogate" is the name of this Sunday. "Rogate" means "pray." So important was the subject of prayer deemed by the Christian Church that she set aside a special Sunday on which it should be especially considered. This is proper. Prayer is the first mark of a Christian. When Saul was converted, we read: "Behold, he prayeth." When the malefactor on the cross had come to faith in the dying Savior, he prayed: "Lord, remember me when Thou comest into Thy kingdom." Where there is breath, there is life; where there is prayer, there is spiritual life. But prayer, the privilege of Christians, is only too often neglected; the necessity of prayer is not always realized; too little is known of what constitutes a true prayer; many erroneous notions regarding it are prevalent. Since all this is but too true, and since Christians need constant exhortation to pray, let us hear to-day

Christ's Instruction on Prayer.

From the text we learn,

1. To whom we should pray.

Christ says: "Whatsoever ye shall ask the Father in My name." The Father, God, is to be called upon. In the time of the godless King Ahab, the Prophet Elijah challenged the priests of Baal, four hundred and fifty in number, to make a test as to who was the true God, Baal or Jehovah. The story is known. You remember that the priests of Baal cried from morning until noon, "O Baal, hear us!" But there was no answer. Elijah mockingly said: "Cry aloud; perhaps your god is on a journey, or he is sleeping and must be awaked; cry aloud!" And they cried aloud, and cut themselves with knives and lancets till the blood gushed out upon them. And they cried till midday, and still there was no answer. Why not? Their prayer was a vain prayer; their god was an idol. Elijah called upon the true God, and He answered.

Now you may say, "Well, these people were heathen; they knew no better." But still this heathenish practise of prayer is carried out to-day in our enlightened land by millions of people. The Roman Catholics call upon the Virgin Mary, upon angels and so-called saints. That is heathenish idolatry; we have no command to call upon them, nor a promise that such prayers will be heard. It is heathenish idolatry to call upon the "All-wise Architect of the Universe," "the Supreme Being," "the Benign Providence," as is done in the lodges. To Christians this is so self-evident that it seems to be a waste of words to speak of it. Christians know that only the true God, Father, Son, and Holy Ghost, is to be called upon, because to Him alone such honor is due, and He alone is able and willing to hear our prayer. Christ says in our text: "Whatsoever ye shall ask the Father in My name." In His combat with Satan He said: "Thou shalt worship the Lord, thy God, and Him only shalt thou serve." And as to the saints, Scripture forbids us to call upon them. "Doubtless, Thou art our Father, though Abraham" — a saint — "be ignorant of us, and Israel" — another saint — "acknowledge us not. Thou, O Lord, art our Father, our Redeemer; Thy name is from everlasting." Is. 63, 16. Only that is a true prayer which is addressed to the Triune God, and only they who believe in this Triune God can pray acceptably, as we shall now see. We ask,

2. Who only can pray?

Christ gives this instruction to His disciples: "Whatsoever ye shall ask the Father in My name." Only Christians know God to be their Father for Christ's sake; only Christians believe on the name of the Son, and approach the Throne of Grace in Jesus' name. Only disciples, Christians, can pray.

An unbeliever cannot pray. His heart is filled with malice against God. He will not pray; he spurns the very suggestion of prayer; to him prayer is an object of ridicule and jest. In times of great calamity — in a *Titanic* disaster, in a San Francisco earthquake, in a Dayton flood — he will cry aloud, "Lord, keep me!" That, however, is nothing but the cry of despair, the cry of the heathen, "Baal, hear us!" For who the true God is the unbeliever knows not. Of such prayers God says: "And when ye spread forth your hands, I will hide Mine eyes from you; yea, when ye make many prayers, I will not hear." Is. 1, 15. Christians only, who through faith in Christ have become children of God, can call upon God as their Father in Jesus' name.

My friend, do you pray? No? And you call yourself a Christian? Impossible! A Christian can and does pray. But since even Christians neglect this privilege only too often, — for their flesh is weak, — and in order to incite them to pray, we ask,

3. What should induce us to pray?

Our text is taken from the Lord's farewell address to His disciples. Among other things He had spoken of trials and tribulations that would befall them after His going to the Father. "Ye shall weep and lament, but the world shall rejoice." Again He said: "In the world ye shall have tribulation." You will have trials and afflictions peculiar to children of God; hence you need aid, comfort, assistance. Therefore remember: "Whatsoever ye shall ask the Father in My name, He will give it you. Ask, and it shall be given you." As a child, when hurt or perplexed, goes to his father or his mother for help and comfort, so we Christians are to cast all our cares upon our heavenly Father. What should induce us to pray? Our wants and necessities.

But the devil endeavors to dissuade us from prayer; he knows what a mighty weapon prayer is in the hands of the Christians, and so he says: "You durst not pray; you are not good enough to pray; you cannot pray; God will not hear you. Postpone it till you have amended your life." When such fiery darts of the Evil One afflict us, let us look to God's command, "Ask, and ye shall receive"; "Call upon Me in the day of trouble." Here is God's command to pray; hence, pray in spite of the devil. Follow the example of David. When he was sorely afflicted on account of his sins, his flesh said, "You durst not pray; God will not hear you." But David, casting aside these insinuations of Satan, approached God pleading: "When Thou saidst, Seek ye My face, my heart said unto Thee, Thy face, Lord, will I seek." Ps. 27, 8. "Seek ye My face," was a command of God meaning, "Pray to Me." This command of God made David bold to pray.

Fellow-Christians, you have needs, spiritual and earthly — pray. The devil is your enemy who hates the prayer of Christians, and tries to hinder it. Listen to God's command, Pray! You have doubts as to your worthiness to pray; fight them down by His grace. Here is His gracious exhortation: "Whatsoever ye shall ask the Father in My name, He will give it you. Ask, and ye shall receive."

4. But now the question arises, *How shall we pray?*

"Whatsoever ye shall ask the Father in My name." Christ speaks to His disciples, to such as believe on Him. Remember, says He, when you address God in prayer, you speak to the Father; you are His children. How did you become such? Through Me. So, when praying, say: This do, Father, for Thy Son's sake, in whom we are made acceptable in Thy sight. Ask Him in My name, not in your own; go to Him relying on My merits, not on your own, and He cannot and will not refuse you. Just as a messenger or an official of a king comes in the name, the authority, of the king and asks a hearing on account of him that sent him, so the Christian prays to God in the name, the authority, of Christ, and is confident of being heard for His sake. "All things," says Scripture in another place, "whatsoever ye ask, *believing,* ye shall receive." To pray in Jesus' name means to pray in faith and firm confidence in Christ's merits. The Pharisee who went into the Temple to pray, relied on his own goodness, and did not go down to his house justified. A Christian says with Daniel: "We do not present our supplications before Thee for our righteousnesses, but for Thy great mercies," and with the publican: "Lord, be merciful to me, a sinner!" Hence all our prayers close thus: This do for Christ Jesus' sake.

5. For what should we pray?

The Lord says: "Whatsoever ye shall ask the Father in My name, He will give it you." There is no burden too great, no burden too small, that you may not cast upon the Lord in prayer. "Cast all your cares upon Him," says Peter to the suffering Christians; and Paul says: "Be careful for nothing; but in everything, by prayer and supplication, with thanksgiving, let your requests be made known unto God."

But we must remember Christ speaks to Christians, who ask in Christ's name. Christians are Christ-minded; they have His spirit. "If any one have not the spirit of Christ, he is none of His." Hence it would be folly to ask for anything and everything, prompted by our whims and fancies. True faith cannot expect, hope, or pray for anything but what God has taught us in His Word to ask for, and what He has promised us. Foolish prayers are not heard. The Lord speaks to Christians, who pray according to His will, submitting their will to God's will. Hence St. John says: "This is the confidence that we have in Him, that, if we ask anything according to His will, He heareth us." A Christian praying in Jesus' name will do as Jesus did. In the Garden of Gethsemane the Savior prayed: "Father, if Thou be willing, remove this cup from Me; nevertheless, not My will, but Thine, be done." And of the leper we read that, upon approaching the Lord, he said: "Lord, if Thou wilt, Thou canst make me clean." So, then, temporal gifts, such as good health, riches, skill, wisdom, and the like, we should ask for with the condition, "If Thou wilt." We are very short-sighted, and oftentimes what we deem to be indispensably necessary would be to our soul's detriment if we did receive it.

But for spiritual gifts, which are absolutely necessary for our soul's salvation, we should ask without condition. Why? We know the will of our Father. He wills our salvation. These things being necessary thereto, He wills to give them. Said the Lord: "If ye, then, being evil, know how to give good gifts unto your children, how much more shall your heavenly Father give the Holy Spirit to them that ask Him?" Hence we pray for these spiritual blessings, such as forgiveness of sins, the grace of God, faith, renewal, guidance of the Holy Spirit, steadfastness in faith, perseverance amid tribulation, without condition.

Praying in this mind and with this sentiment, we pray in Jesus' name and are sure of being heard. Why? Because we have His promise.

6. What is the promise?

"Verily, verily, I say unto you, Whatsoever ye shall ask the Father in My name, He will give it you. Ask, and ye shall receive."

Here the Lord not only makes the promise that the Father will grant our petition, but He repeats the promise and confirms it with an oath: "Verily, verily." Can we doubt His promise? Who is He? Our Savior and our God. Upon His promises we may and ought to rely. To doubt them would be calling God a liar. These promises we should believe in spite of the cavilings of our reason, and in spite of such experiences as would seem to prove the contrary. It not infrequently happens that we pray for a certain thing, but fail to get it. How prone are we then to assume that our prayer has not been heard! Reason's logic seems plausible and irrefutable, but still it is false. If we ask anything according to His will, God will and must hear us, otherwise He would reject His own Son, our Savior. No, God does not break His promises; our prayers in faith are acceptable and heard. And if God does not give us precisely what we asked for, He grants us something better in its place. When the Apostle Paul three times humbly besought the Lord to take a certain heavy burden from him, he was told: "My grace is sufficient for thee; for My strength is made perfect in weakness." Paul did not think his prayer had not been heard, but was quite satisfied to have Jesus' strength and grace. Again, the Lord often delays answering our prayers for a merciful purpose. At Cana He said: "Mine hour is not yet come." "Not yet" — but it will come.

It remains forever true: God hears every prayer of the Christian. Abraham prayed, and God answered. Jacob prayed, and God answered. Moses asked, and God answered. Elijah prayed, and God answered. David prayed, and God answered. Daniel prayed, and God answered. Peter, the centurion, Luther, hosts of Christians, prayed, and God answered. You prayed, and God answered. Hence, ask, seek, knock. "Ask, and He will give it you." Ask for increase of faith, and you will receive it. Ask for removal of doubt, and your doubts will be removed. Ask for steadfastness in faith, and it shall be granted. Ask for a blessed end, and you will attain it. "Ask that your joy may be made full." Amen.

The Doctrine of Holy Baptism.

MATT. 28, 19. 20.

And Jesus came and spake unto them, saying, All power is given unto Me in heaven and in earth. Go ye, therefore, and disciple all nations, baptizing them into the name of the Father and of the Son and of the Holy Ghost; teaching them to observe all things whatsoever I have commanded you. And, lo, I am with you alway, even unto the end of the world.

This is the Last Great Commission of our Lord to His disciples. He was about to ascend into heaven; His disciples were to go out into the world to wage war against the formidable kingdom of Satan, to destroy its bulwarks, and upon its ruins to plant the cross, the emblem of the Crucified One. What a task! But Jesus, their King, consoles and strengthens them. "Ye ambassadors of Mine, fear not ye. Though you will no longer enjoy My visible presence, invisibly I shall be with you, guide you, protect you in the performance of your sacred calling. I am the King of heaven and earth; I possess all power. Go ye, therefore, to your great task undaunted. Disciple the nations, build My Church. With My grace and My mighty power I shall assist you. Disciple the nations, baptizing them, teaching them."

This His devoted disciples did, and the work is still being carried on to-day, and will be carried on till the last day. Then the scaffold of this world will be torn down; the holy Christian Church will be complete.

The central thought of Christ's Great Commission is: *"Disciple the nations."* How is it to be done? How are disciples, believers in Christ, made? The Lord says there are two means: by *baptizing* them and by *teaching* them.

My purpose to-day is to speak to you on Baptism. The text answers all essential questions pertaining thereto. In the time allotted to a sermon, this doctrine can be presented in outline only. A fuller treatment of the several parts may be reserved for another time. So my topic for to-day, based on the solemn charge of our Master, is:

The Doctrine of Holy Baptism.

1. Who instituted Holy Baptism?

In our text we have the divine command of Christ: "Go ye, therefore, and disciple all nations, *baptizing* them." Baptism is instituted by God. True, John the Baptist baptized before this general command was given; but from whom did he derive his authority? St. Luke informs us that "the word of God," the command of God, "came unto John in the wilderness." What was the import of this "word of God"? We read: "John came into all the country about Jordan, preaching the baptism of repentance for the remission of sins." And John himself says in that great testimony of his regarding the Christ: "He," God, "sent me to baptize with water." The Baptist derived his authority to baptize from God. Between the baptism of John and that of Christ there is no essential difference: John baptized unto Him that was to come; Christian baptism is unto Him that has come. Baptism is a divine institution.

2. What is the visible element in Baptism?

This is not expressly mentioned in our text. Why not? Because it was universally known to be water. The Lord simply says: *"Baptize* them in the name of the Father," etc. The disciples full well understood this word "baptize" to connote baptize with *water,* just as we to-day, when we say, *"Wash* your face," understand that not milk or wine is to be used, but water. Hence it was unnecessary for our Lord to specify: "Baptize with water."

John the Baptist expressly says: God "sent me to baptize with *water."* Of him, too, we read that he "baptized in Aenon, near to Salim, because there was much *water* there." In His conversation with Nicodemus, Jesus, speaking of Baptism, says: "Except a man be born of water and of the Spirit, he cannot enter into the kingdom of God." So throughout the New Testament we find that water, common, simple water, is the visible element of this Sacrament.

Why is it necessary to prove such a self-evident fact from the Scriptures? Because men in the name of religion have now and then substituted milk, wine, or some other liquid, and have called it a baptism. This is wrong. There is no baptism where water, simple water, is not used.

3. How is Baptism to be administered?

"Baptize them in the name of the Father and of the Son and of the Holy Ghost," says the text. Here we have the express formula to be used. The candidate for baptism is to be baptized "in the name of the Father and of the Son and of the Holy Ghost." These words must not be changed; Christ prescribed them. The words, moreover, contain a confession of faith. Observe that the text says: "Baptize them into the *name,"* not "baptize them into the *names* of the Father," etc. That means that there is but

one name, *one* essence in God; there is but *one* God, but
three distinct Persons: Father, Son, and Holy Ghost.
Our God is the Triune God. In the name and by authority
of this Triune God, Baptism is to be performed. And
when Christ commands: *"Baptize* them in the name," etc.,
that means that water is to be applied to the person to be
baptized, either by sprinkling or pouring water upon him,
or by immersing him in water. The mode of the application of water is indifferent, because no definite rule therefor
has been laid down. The Baptists insist on immersion,
i. e., putting the whole body under water. This mode of
baptizing, immersion, is valid; but the Baptists are wrong
in maintaining that immersion is the only right way, and
in rejecting all other baptisms.

4. What is the benefit of Baptism?

The command reads: "Baptize them *into* the name of
the Father," etc. This phrase *"into* the name" has a deep
significance. It does not merely mean: Baptize them by
authority of the Triune God, but *"into"* denotes entrance,
it denotes coming into fellowship with the Triune God.
"Baptize *into* the name" makes the promise and gives the
assurance that the person who before baptism was without
God now, by baptism, has entered into relationship with
God, has become a child of God. Is that true? Christ
says so. He says: *"Disciple* the nations, baptizing them."
How does one become a disciple of Christ? By Baptism.
Who is a disciple of Christ? An adherent, a follower of
Christ, a believer in Christ. "Disciple the nations, bap-
tizing them," means that Baptism generates faith in the
person baptized; for without faith no one can be a dis-
ciple of Christ.

Hear how highly St. Paul extols Baptism. To the
Galatians he writes: "Ye are all the children of God by
faith in Christ Jesus; for as many of you as have been

baptized into Christ have put on Christ." By Baptism we enter into union with Christ, we put on Christ, the benefits of Christ's redemption become our own, we become thereby the children of God by faith in Christ Jesus. St. Peter speaks in equally high terms of Baptism when he says to his pentecostal hearers: "Repent and be baptized, every one of you, for the remission of sins." Baptism is a means of grace, through which forgiveness of sins is granted by God Himself. "Baptism doth also now save us," says Peter in his First Epistle, and, explaining how it saves, he says: "Not the putting away of the filth of the flesh," — Baptism is not an outward purifier or a ceremonial washing, — "but" Baptism is "the answer," the compact, "of a good conscience toward God." Briefly: By Baptism we come into covenant relation with God, the effect of which is a good conscience, so that our sins no longer can condemn us. God is our Father; we, His children. Such a gracious water of life is Baptism.

But how can water do such great things? Common water can never take away the filth of the soul; baptismal water, however, is "not simple water only, but water connected with the word of God." Baptism is, as St. Paul says, "the washing of water by the word." It is water in conjunction with the word of God. This word of God makes baptismal water so powerful. Matthew in our text explicitly gives the *commandment* of Christ: "Baptize them"; and the *promise* of grace is implied in the words: *"Disciple* the nations, *baptizing* them." Elsewhere the promise is explicitly stated thus: "He that believeth and is baptized shall be saved." So the word of God, His command and His promise, communicates such great power to Baptism. —

To illustrate. The water of the Jordan had no power in itself to cleanse from leprosy, but when Naaman, the leper, was bidden by the Lord through the mouth of His prophet Elisha to wash in the Jordan seven times, and he did so, he was cleansed of his leprosy. Why? Because the word of God imparted that power to the water. When Christ said to the lepers, "Be clean!" they were cleansed. Why? Because of the powerful word of God. Again, Gideon, in the name of the Lord, conquered the hosts of the Midianites with three hundred men armed with pitchers, torches, and trumpets. Why? Because of the command of God. So all depends on the word of God. Why does the earth bring forth grass to this day? Because of God's blessing: "Let the earth bring forth grass." This water does such great things because God's word is connected therewith. This we believe. "Reason," says Luther, "can never understand how Baptism is a washing of regeneration, but what God says is true, whether my senses corroborate it or not. He is omnipotent and can fulfil His word."

5. To whom is Baptism to be applied?

"Go ye, therefore, and disciple all *nations,* baptizing them." "Nations" are made up of men, women, and children. These are to be baptized, and these only. It is a sacrilege practised by the Roman Catholic Church to baptize bells; it is a travesty upon this sacred act to "baptize" ships with wine.

That men and women are to be baptized is generally conceded. The question is: Should children be baptized? Children belong to a nation, aye, they make up the greater part of a nation; hence, as long as this general command, "Baptize all nations," holds good, so long, we maintain, children are to be baptized. This command, being so general, is proof, positive, incontrovertible proof, for the baptism of infants. We need no other. But corroboration of this truth we find amply in the Scriptures. After Peter's great pentecostal sermon the hearers "were pricked

in their hearts, and said unto Peter and the rest of the
apostles, 'Men and brethren, what shall we do?'" Peter
answered: "Repent and be baptized, every one of you, in
the name of Jesus Christ for the remission of sins, and ye
shall receive the gift of the Holy Ghost. For the promise
is unto you *and to your children."* The household baptisms
recorded in the New Testament prove the same thing.
Paul "baptized Lydia," a seller of purple, "and *her household."* The keeper of the prison at Philippi was "baptized,
and *all his."* Paul baptized the *household* of Stephanas.
Is it not plain as plain can be that such expressions as
"household" and "all his" are specially used to include the
little ones of the family circle?

*6. Is Baptism to be administered indiscriminately, to
old and young alike?*

The text says: "Go ye, therefore, and disciple all
nations, baptizing them, . . . teaching them."

The charge is: *"Make disciples* of all nations." How
many means are there to make disciples? Two. Which?
By baptizing them and by teaching them. The text does
not say: First baptize, then teach. Christ says both should
be done, each at the proper time. How did the disciples
understand the Master's injunction? The hearers at Pentecost were first taught by Peter and, "having gladly received
the Word, were baptized." Lydia was first instructed, then
baptized; the keeper of the prison at Philippi likewise.
So this was the practise of the Church in regard to adults.
Thus the command of the Master was understood and
carried out by His disciples. — Now, as to children. They,
too, are to be made disciples. They cannot be taught.
They are flesh born of the flesh, and stand in need of
regeneration. They are to be made disciples by the only
means of regeneration applicable to them — Baptism.
The objection so often heard: Can children believe? is

clearly met by the positive declaration of our Lord Himself, who speaks of "these little ones which believe in Me." How their faith is constituted is none of our business.

Hence our practise is founded on the teaching of our Lord and His disciples. Little children are baptized and thus regenerated; adults we first instruct, and when they profess faith, begotten by the Word, we baptize them in accordance with the dictum of our Lord: "He that believeth and is baptized shall be saved." To adults, Baptism is a seal of their covenant relation with God, greatly strengthening their faith.

7. Who is to administer Baptism?

"Go ye, therefore, and disciple all nations, baptizing them, . . . teaching them." To whom does Christ say: "Go ye"? To His disciples. Only disciples can make disciples. How many were there to whom He spoke? Eleven, for Judas, the traitor, had gone to his place. Were these the only ones for whom this solemn charge was intended? No. All disciples of Christ are so commissioned. How do we know? The Master said: "Lo, I am with you alway, even unto the end of the world." Baptism was thus made a permanent institution of the Church to the end of days. These eleven died, but the charge to make disciples is valid even to-day.

Who is to carry out this command of the Master? His disciples. By His grace we are His disciples. We have the privilege and the power to administer Baptism. Every Christian congregation and every member of such congregation possesses this power. Why, then, do not the individual Christians baptize their children? Because God is a God of order. The rule to obtain in the Church is: "Let all things be done decently and in order." The Christian congregations have called ministers of Christ to whom they have delegated this power to perform Baptism in their name. As Paul says: "Let a man so account of us as of the ministers of Christ and stewards of the mysteries of God."

But in case of extreme necessity, when it is impossible to summon the minister, or where there is danger that the child may die before his arrival, any Christian has the right to administer Baptism, and hence, in your hymn-books you will find a formula for that very purpose. The minister, later on, makes inquiry how Baptism was applied and duly records it, so that the child in after years may rest assured of his having been validly baptized.

In conclusion. It is Christ who saves us. What He has gained for all He offers to all in the Gospel. And what He thus offers to all He grants to the individuals in Baptism. The infant is regenerated by Baptism; the adult believer's faith is wonderfully strengthened by Baptism, since it is the personal application of the Gospel-assurance of the forgiveness of sins.

What an abundance of grace God showers upon us to counteract the sting of sin! The Gospel assures us of pardon; the Lord's Supper assures us of pardon; the covenant of grace made with God in our infancy assures us of pardon. In hours of affliction when our conscience would condemn us, let us flee to these fountains of God's grace and become refreshed. When Satan accuses us of having departed from the Lord, let us also look back to our baptismal covenant, knowing that our merciful God says: "The mountains shall depart, and the hills be removed; but My kindness shall not depart from thee, neither shall the covenant of My peace be removed, saith the Lord that hath mercy on thee." Amen.

The Various Grades of Brotherly Admonition.

MATT. 18, 15—18.

Moreover, if thy brother shall trespass against thee, go and tell him his fault between thee and him alone. If he shall hear thee, thou hast gained thy brother. But if he will not hear thee, then take with thee one or two more, that in the mouth of two or three witnesses every word may be established. And if he shall neglect to hear them, tell it unto the church; but if he neglect to hear the church, let him be unto thee as an heathen man and a publican. Verily, I say unto you, Whatsoever ye shall bind on earth shall be bound in heaven; and whatsoever ye shall loose on earth shall be loosed in heaven.

A Christian duty, only too often neglected, is that of brotherly admonition. What do we understand by brotherly admonition? If one knows his brother to be living in sin, it is the manifest duty of the Christian to try to reclaim his brother from damnation by showing him from the Word of God the gravity, the damnableness of his sin. An immortal soul, bought by the blood of Christ, is in danger of being lost!

And this duty of endeavoring to save a brother's soul is often neglected? Sorry to say, yes. You see a brother venturing into a treacherous stream; you warn him. Why? He may lose his life. You see him handling a gun recklessly; you warn him. Why? He may lose his life. You see him nearing a dangerous precipice; you warn him. Why? He may lose his life. And you see him sinning, you know that he is in danger of losing life eternal, and you will not warn him? Is that acting brotherly towards him? "No, it is not," you admit. But is not eternal life worth infinitely more than this temporal life? "True," you answer; "but the common experience is this: Whereas I gain the gratitude of the brother whom

I have warned against losing his life by entering the treacherous stream, by handling the gun carelessly, etc., I generally incur his bitter hatred by admonishing him of his sin." Very true; flesh and blood is so perverse. But does this fact do away with your Christian duty?

The Lord says: *"Tell him his fault."* And the purpose? How glorious! — to gain the brother. Let us to-day learn anew our Master's will, and let us ask Him for a courageous heart to carry out this difficult, but blessed work. Under the guidance of God's Holy Spirit let us consider the subject agreeably to our text:

The Various Grades of Brotherly Admonition.

1.

"If thy brother shall trespass against thee, go and tell him his fault between thee and him alone. If he shall hear thee, thou hast gained thy brother."

To whom does the Lord speak? To the brethren of a trespassing brother. Who are "brethren"? All that belong to the "church," the local congregation, all that partake of the Lord's Supper with us — men, women, youths, maidens.

What is the nature of the sin that is subject to church-discipline? "If thy brother shall *trespass* against thee." Trespass is sin. Now, is every sin of the brother the object of a brotherly admonition? No. By trespass is not meant any and every sin that is inevitable even with the best Christian, owing to the sinful flesh that adheres to him even unto death. The admonition has as its purpose to *gain* the brother, hence the "trespass against thee," the sin on account of which he is to be admonished, has caused him to fall from grace. If repentance does not follow, the brother is *lost*. It is a sin on account of which we ultimately, if the brother is not "gained," must look upon

him as "an heathen man and a publican." St. Paul writes
to the Corinthians: "I have written unto you not to keep
company if any man that is called a brother be a fornicator, or covetous, or an idolater, or a railer, or a drunkard,
or an extortioner; with such an one no not to eat." 1 Cor.
5, 11. This, of course, does not exhaust the list of sins
that subject to church-discipline. That cannot be done.
Any sin which may finally cause the brother to lose his
soul is a "trespass against *thee.*"

But how am I to understand this phrase, "trespass
against thee"? That does not say that you must be the
direct object of this sin, that wrong must have been done
you personally, but a sin "against thee" is one that is
secret as yet, but of which you have knowledge. The
brother is living in a sin that actually in God's sight puts
him on a level with "an heathen man and a publican."
You know of it. A sin known "between you and him
alone," which puts the brother's soul in jeopardy, is a sin
"against thee."

Now, *"if thy brother shall trespass against thee,"* what?
Pay no heed to it? No. *"Go and tell him his fault."*
In what spirit should you go? Why, in the spirit of a
brother. Love for his immortal soul should impel you to
go and tell him his fault. With what end in view should
this brotherly admonition be carried out? To gain the
brother. *"Thou hast gained thy brother"* — this thought
dominates the entire instruction of our Lord. The brother
is in danger of losing his soul eternally; reclaim him from
destruction; "gain thy brother." Love for the sinning
brother is to be the only motive and guide in dealing with
him. The love of Christ, who shed His blood also for this
erring brother, is to impel you to convince him of the
error of his way. In the preceding context the Lord speaks
of His seeking love towards sinners. And how great is
His joy when the lost sheep is found! This is the senti-

ment that should govern you, govern us all, when administering brotherly admonition. "Go and tell him his fault *between thee and him alone.*" As yet the sin is not public. Only you and he know about it. Hence let the admonition be "between thee and him alone." Love does not delight in spreading the brother's misdeeds; love delights in *gaining* the brother. "Tell him his fault" in a brotherly love; call the fault a fault, sin; show him the gravity thereof by the Word of God; tell him of his Savior, whose will is not that he should perish, but that he should come to repentance. The motive to gain the brother, the impelling force, love towards the erring brother, will by God's grace prompt the proper words to reach the sinner's heart. If you succeed, what? *"Thou hast gained thy brother."* Rejoice, thank and praise God, because an immortal soul has been wrested from Satan's clutches. But otherwise the whole matter is to be buried, so the object has been attained; your lips must be sealed; not a word about the matter is to be even whispered to a third person.

2.

But if you do not succeed, love to your brother impels you to go farther. The text says: *"But if he will not hear thee, then take with thee one or two more, that in the mouth of two or three witnesses every word may be established."* The Lord says: If, after repeated efforts on your part to convince the brother of his fault, you are, nevertheless, unsuccessful, then take one or two other brethren of the congregation with thee to speak with the erring brother. The brother's sin is not to receive undue publicity; only one or two are to be told thereof. Whom are you to select? Not men whom he may imagine to have a grudge against him. That very fact would close his heart against all admonition. Wisdom, love, dictates that friends of his should be selected. And these friends are not only to be reliable witnesses of what is said and done, but they, too, should add their earnest exhortations and entreaties. This, if anything, should open the sinner's eyes to the gravity of the situation. If his friends, his best friends, warn him of the wrath of God; if they, bound by the love of God, impelled by the love for his soul, must tell him that, if he persists in his sin, they can no longer look upon him as a brother, as a child of God, but as a victim of Satan, — this, if anything, should melt his hardened heart and lead him to repentance and amendment of life.

This effort, if futile, should be repeated so long as there is hope of gaining the brother. If successful, well and good — "thou hast gained thy brother." Drop the matter, seal your lips, praise God. There is joy in heaven over one sinner that repenteth.

3.

If this second grade of admonition should prove a failure, love constrains you to go still farther, to take the last available means to save the brother's soul from damnation — you must bring the matter before the congregation.

The text reads: *"And if he shall neglect to hear them, tell it unto the church."* — The "church" here comprises those that "assemble in His name," v. 20; hence it is the local congregation. This is the highest court of appeal. Here, again, every effort possible to gain the brother is to be made. What an impression the united entreaties and exhortations must make upon the sinner! How hardened the heart of such a one must be if the exhortation of the entire congregation should not cause him to repent of his sin. Thanks be to God, many and many a lost sheep has thus been brought back again into the arms of the Savior!

But even this brotherly admonition of the entire congregation may fail. What then is to be done?

4.

"But if he neglect to hear the church, let him be unto thee as an heathen man and a publican." In other words, such a one is no longer to be looked upon as a brother, but is to be expelled from the Christian congregation. St. Paul says: "Put away from among yourselves that wicked person." 1 Cor. 5, 13. Where the church thus pronounces the ban, she is in fact doing nothing else than pronouncing the sentence that God had long before pronounced against him because of his sin. "Let him be unto thee as an heathen man and a publican." Before God he was such long ago.

This expulsion from the congregation has for its object not so much to get rid of the person fallen into grievous sin, but, in the last analysis, this, too, is an act of love; it is the last resort to open the sinner's eyes to the abyss of his guilt in order to gain him. St. Paul says 1 Cor. 5, 5, regarding the fornicator, that the congregation should "deliver such an one unto Satan for the destruction of the flesh, that the spirit may be saved in the day of the Lord Jesus Christ." But in like manner as he had demanded the expulsion of the sinner from the congregation, so earnestly he also demanded his readmittance when the ban had had the desired result, the brother having repented of his sin and thus having been gained. 2 Cor. 2, 5—11.

Alarmed by the earnestness of his former brethren, who must go so far as to sever all churchly connection with him, — because of love for his immortal soul, because of due regard to Christ's command, and for a testimony to them without, — the erring brother may penitently return to Christ and the church. And what the church thus does in Christ's name is valid before our Father in heaven. Christ assures us in the continuation of our text: "Verily I say unto you, Whatsoever ye shall bind on earth shall be bound in heaven; and whatsoever ye shall loose on earth shall be loosed in heaven."

In conclusion let it be repeated that the object of church-discipline is to *gain the brother*. If this be kept in view, we shall readily see that the Lord speaks of three *kinds* of admonition. We are not to hurry from one grade of admonition to the other; we are not to put the erring brother under the auctioneer's hammer — one, two, three! The various grades of brotherly admonition are to be repeated as long as there is hope that he may be gained thereby, or till it become manifest that he obstinately refuses to heed the Word of God.

Because the object of church-discipline is to gain the brother, we should go to him at an opportune time. When we observe that the brother whom we are to admonish is ruffled, irritated, when matters have gone wrong in his family or in his business, it is no time to "tell him his fault"; let us bide our time. When Adam sinned, God waited; He came to him in the cool of the evening.

The object is to gain the brother. Let us go to him, therefore, in the proper attitude of mind. In our closets let us first humble ourselves before our God, look upon ourselves in the light of the Law, see our own great sins and the greater Savior. Thus we shall go to the erring brother as redeemed sinners, filled with the love of Christ, seeking to save that which is lost.

God grant that the testimony of Paul to the Roman Christians may apply to us: "I am persuaded of you, my brethren, that ye also are full of goodness, filled with all knowledge, able also to admonish one another." Amen.

St. Paul's Instruction Regarding the Lord's Supper.

1 Cor. 11, 23—29.

For I have received of the Lord that which also I delivered unto you, That the Lord Jesus, the same night in which He was betrayed, took bread; and when He had given thanks, He brake it and said, Take, eat; this is My body, which is broken for you: this do in remembrance of Me. After the same manner also He took the cup when He had supped, saying, This cup is the new testament in My blood; this do ye, as oft as ye drink it, in remembrance of Me. For as often as ye eat this bread and drink this cup, ye do show the Lord's death till He come. Wherefore, whosoever shall eat this bread, and drink this cup of the Lord, unworthily, shall be guilty of the body and blood of the Lord. But let a man examine himself, and so let him eat of that bread and drink of that cup. For he that eateth and drinketh unworthily eateth and drinketh damnation to himself, not discerning the Lord's body.

What is the Sacrament of the Altar? The Lutheran, *i. e.,* the Biblical, answer is this: "It is the true body and blood of our Lord Jesus Christ under the bread and wine, for us Christians to eat and to drink, instituted by Christ Himself."

No doctrine of the Lutheran Church has been more subject to controversy in the Protestant Churches than that of the Lord's Supper. Why it should be so is almost incomprehensible. The words of Scripture regarding this doctrine are so plain, so simple, that a child can readily grasp their meaning. Why, then, has this doctrine been made such a fierce battle-ground? Because it can be assailed with arguments appealing plausibly to reason. But is reason the judge of divine matters? In theory all Protestant Churches hold with Luther: "The Word of God shall fix articles of faith, none else, not even an angel from heaven"; but in practise the Lutheran Church alone carries out this principle. Again and again the denominations outside the Lutheran Church allow themselves to be tripped into error by asking the question, How can this be? How can water in Baptism do such great things? How can the Lord give us His body and blood in the Lord's Supper? How can Christ even to-day be with us invisibly as the God-man? Everlastingly it is how? how? And because they cannot grasp the *how* with their reason, they refuse to accept the teachings of the Bible.

Here is their fundamental error. If they would carry out this principle consistently, they should ask, How can Christ be God and man in one person? How can there be but one God, and yet three distinct persons? How can the dead rise on the latter day? Where would they finally land? In the realm of the heathen religion, the religion of natural man. But then, too, they might throw their Bibles into the fire, and close their houses of worship. Thanks be to God, they are thus far preserved through the mercy of God from carrying out their false principle consistently.

The Lutheran doctrine of the Lord's Supper, mysterious and incomprehensible though it may be, is true, because the Bible, God's Word, so teaches. That settles the matter. God speaks; we are to hear and believe. That is the attitude of the Lutheran Church towards the Bible, and hence also to the teaching of this doctrine. Assuming this attitude, the doctrine as such is not difficult of comprehension. How do we learn of it? We collect all the passages of Holy Writ treating of this matter, and simply record the facts, "So says the Lord." Do we find mysteries here? Yes, but — "so says the Lord." If there were no mysteries in the Scriptures, we should need no Bible, for then our mind would be just as great as that of God. No, we follow the injunction of the apostle, "bringing into captivity every thought to the obedience of Christ," knowing that, by adhering to His Word, we are, as He Himself says, "His disciples indeed."

Now, then, what does Scripture say regarding the Lord's Supper? We have four records of this divine institution, one in Matt. 26, another in Mark 14, a third in Luke 22, and the fourth in 1 Cor. 11. The words used in all four records are almost precisely the same. One record would have been sufficient, but to make assurance more than doubly and trebly sure, the Holy Ghost has seen fit to record this institution of our blessed Lord four times. Does not that very fact show how important this doctrine is?

We have chosen the passage from 1 Cor. 11 for our text. Upon the basis of this text let us consider:

St. Paul's Instruction Regarding the Lord's Supper.

1. Who is the author of the Lord's Supper?

We read: *"For I have received of the Lord that which also I delivered unto you, That the Lord Jesus, the same night in which He was betrayed, took bread; and when He had given thanks, He brake it and said, Take, eat; this is My body, which is broken for you: this do in remembrance of Me."* The Corinthians had need of a thorough instruction in this doctrine, the reasons for which we cannot enlarge upon just now, since the subject-matter is of prime importance to-day.

Observe the solemn manner in which the Apostle introduces his instruction: *"I received of the Lord that which I also delivered unto you."* "Corinthian Christians," says the Apostle, "I *delivered* this doctrine unto you, I instructed you thoroughly in it, hence you ought to know it. But your conduct just now shows that you have forgotten it, or else you are shamefully abusing it. Be it known to you, therefore, that the doctrine which I delivered unto you is not mine. I am an apostle of Jesus Christ. Whatsoever I preach unto you I preach not in my own name, but in the name of my Lord. And especially of this doctrine — to show you its great importance I solemnly affirm: 'I have received it *of the Lord,*' that is to say, I have received a special revelation regarding it from the Lord Jesus Christ Himself, who instituted it. So you can rely upon my every word as coming from the Lord Jesus Himself."

Why this solemn introduction? Aye, why did the Lord vouchsafe to Paul a special revelation of this doctrine? All the words of Paul are God's Word, written by inspiration of the Holy Ghost; but here the Lord Jesus Himself grants Paul a special revelation. Why? To preserve the Church from every possible error. St. Paul, it is assumed, wrote a considerable time after the ascension of our Lord. He did not copy his doctrine from others, nor did he receive it from men, as he expressly says, Gal. 1, 12: "For I neither received it of man, neither was I taught it, but by the revelation of Jesus Christ." Now, the Evangelists Matthew, Mark, and Luke record the doctrine of the Lord's Supper in words almost identical with those of Paul. If it had been intended that the words of the Evangelists should be understood differently from what they read, they would have been properly interpreted by Paul, in order to preserve the Church from error. But no! The Lord Jesus, the Institutor of the Sacrament, reveals to Paul the same doctrine that the Evangelists record.

And who is this Lord Jesus? He is, as Paul writes to the Romans, "God over all," aye, as Isaiah says, "the mighty God," who has ways and means to do that which He promises. He is the God-man, who has a body and blood that He can give. He is Truth itself, and therefore cannot lie. When He says, "This is My body," He speaks truly. He is the All-wise, who, looking down through the ages of time, knew that contentions would arise with respect to this ordinance, and therefore He used plain, unmistakable words, so that whosoever is of the truth and will hearken to His words can know the truth. He is, furthermore, the Almighty, who is able to do and give what He has promised.

2. When did Jesus institute the Last Supper?

"The Lord Jesus, the same night in which He was betrayed, took bread." In that solemn night, a few hours before He suffered and died for the sins of the world, the Savior instituted this Sacrament as a rich legacy to His disciples and all Christians. It was His last will. *"This is My body; this is My blood"* — these words have the force and authority of such a document, of a last will or testament. In a matter of such weighty importance, instituted at such a solemn time, our Lord would use plain words. Figurative words, ambiguous words, have no place in a testament. Paul says of a man's testament: "Brethren, I speak after the manner of men. Though it be but a man's covenant, yet, if it be confirmed, no man disannulleth or addeth thereto." Gal. 3, 15. So sacred a man's testament is held to be; but, sad to say, when the Lord of lords and King of kings makes a testament, there are sacrilegious hands trying to destroy it.

3. What is the essence of the Lord's Supper?

"The Lord Jesus, the same night in which He was betrayed, took bread; and when He had given thanks, He brake it and said, *Take, eat; this is My body, which is broken for you:* this do in remembrance of Me. After the same manner also He took the cup, when He had supped, saying, *This cup is the new testament in My blood;* this do ye, as oft as ye drink it, in remembrance of Me. For as often as ye eat this bread and drink this cup, ye do show the Lord's death till He come. Wherefore, *whosoever shall eat this bread, and drink this cup of the Lord, unworthily, shall be guilty of the body and blood of the Lord.* But let a man examine himself, and so let him eat of that bread and drink of that cup. *For he that eateth and drinketh unworthily eateth and drinketh damnation to himself, not discerning the Lord's body."* After the ordinary meal the Lord takes bread, gives thanks, thus separating it from the ordinary use, and says: "Take, eat; this is My body," indicating that something more exalted than ordinary bread was given to them, and likewise with the cup containing wine.

"It is plain that two objects are here spoken of as being present. One is the body and blood of Christ, the other is bread and wine. The body and blood are the invisible, divine elements, while the bread and wine are the visible, earthly elements. The relation of the two elements is that the earthly is the means of the heavenly. That is, by using or appropriating this bread and this wine, the body and blood of Christ are received and appropriated by the communicant." Let us inspect the words: *"This is My body."* The word *"is,"* according to the plain, natural understanding, does not mean "signifies" or "represents" in any language of the civilized world, but *is* shows that something really exists. *"Body"* means a true essential body, not an apparent body; and to remove all doubt, the Lord says: *"My* body." That does away with all figurative language, and to cut off all subterfuges, the Lord adds: "This is My body, *which is broken for you."* If any words in human speech are plain, these are.

The Lord does not say: "This is My *changed* body," as if the bread were changed into the body of Christ, which is the Roman Catholic error of Transubstantiation, and upon which they have built that horrible doctrine of the so-called Mass, upon which again the whole papal system rests. Further proof of the correctness of our version we have in the text. Christ says: "For as often as ye eat *this bread* and drink *this cup*"; again: "Whosoever shall eat this *bread* and drink this *cup*." He speaks of the elements after consecration, and still he says, "this bread" and "this cup." Hence there is no change of the elements. The bread remains bread, and the wine remains wine.

Nor are the divine and the earthly elements separated, so that the body and blood are not received where the bread and wine are taken, — which is the error of other Protestant Churches, — but the two are combined in an inseparable and yet unmixed union. Proof of this we find here also, v. 29 : "For he that eateth and drinketh unworthily eateth and drinketh damnation to himself, *not discerning the Lord's body.*" So the Lord's body is present, but not discerned by such as partake of the Sacrament unworthily. Again, v. 27: "Whosoever shall eat this bread, and drink this cup, unworthily, shall be *guilty of the body and blood of the Lord.*" Nothing can be plainer than that the body and blood of Christ are present, otherwise those partaking unworthily of the Supper could not be guilty thereof.

The same apostle says 1 Cor. 10, 16: "The cup of blessing which we bless, is it not the communion of the blood of Christ? The bread which we break, is it not the communion of the body of Christ?" Since there is a communion of the two, they must be present. Based on this and other plain scriptures, the Lutheran doctrine is this: In, with, and under the bread and wine the communicants receive the true body and blood of our Lord Jesus Christ. God says so. We believe that God's power is equal to His word, and what He says He can do. How this is done, we know not. "We are only asked to believe the fact; the manner is and remains incomprehensible. We have to do with the *what;* the *how* we leave to God."

During that colloquy concerning the Lord's Supper between Zwingli and Luther at Marburg, Luther took a piece of chalk and wrote before him on the table the words of Christ: "This is My body," and successfully defended the doctrine against all arguments adduced to distort these words. Such is the Lutheran attitude over against the Word of God.

At another time Luther said: "My dear Lord Jesus Christ, a terrible dispute has arisen about Thy language in the Holy Supper. Some maintain that Thy words are to be understood in a sense different from that which the words convey. But since these men teach me nothing certain, but only raise doubts in my mind, and neither will nor can prove their position, I will stick to Thy text, just as the words read. If there is anything dark in them, it was Thy will that it should be so; for Thou hast given no other explanation of them, nor commanded it to be done." And again: "They want to know *how* Christ's body is in the bread, and if it cannot be explained to them, they deny its presence; and yet these same men do not know how they open their mouths, move their tongues, or grasp their pens with their hands. I will not say anything about their not knowing how they see, hear, speak, or live. All these things we constantly observe, and yet we do not know how they are brought about; — yet they want to know how Christ's body is in the bread and will not let Christ be the Master."

4. Why did Christ institute this Sacrament?

In connection with the doctrine of the Lord's Supper this is one of the main questions to be answered. But since my purpose to-day is to prove the real presence, and since the question of the benefit of the Lord's Supper is dwelt upon again and again in the confessional sermons, I shall speak of this topic but briefly.

In many Protestant Churches you will find the inscription carved on the communion table: "This do in remembrance of Me," thereby indicating that to them the Lord's Supper is nothing but a memorial. They overlook one or two things. *"This do,"* said the Lord. Do what? Consecrate bread and wine, and under the consecrated bread and wine eat and drink His body and blood *for the forgiveness of sins.* *"This do,"* and when we do this, we remember at the same time that Christ gave His body and blood for the salvation of the world. Then *"we do show the Lord's death,"* v. 26. That implies the main purpose for which the Lord instituted this Sacrament. What is that? *"For the remission of sins,"* as the Evangelists plainly say. The Apostle in our text corroborates this by warning Christians not to partake unworthily of the Lord's Supper; for then they would "eat and drink damnation to themselves." Not for damnation, however, but for salvation was it instituted. Hence, says he, *"let a man examine himself, and so,"* after strict examination of his attitude towards God, *"let him eat of that bread and drink of that cup."* "Examine himself." What does that mean? Examine yourself in the mirror of the Law of God. Are you a sinner? Yes. Do you tremble before the wrath of God on account of your manifold transgressions? Yes. What is your only consolation? That Jesus Christ died for me and shed His blood for me. Do you always firmly believe this? My faith is oftentimes weak. To strengthen this your weak faith, the Lord has instituted His Holy Supper. Here He says to you: As surely as I here give you My body and blood to eat and to drink, so surely you shall believe that I have died for you, you individually, for the remission of your sins. This believe; this saith He that cannot lie. — And since our faith needs frequent strengthening, we should go often to partake of the Lord's Supper. The Apostle considers this to be self-evident; hence he says: "As *often* as ye eat this bread," etc.

We must close. Our text is too rich; we could not do justice to it in one discourse. The Lutheran Biblical doctrine, as you see, is plain, clear. Only because it has been befogged and beclouded by gainsayers who ask, "How can this be?" has it become necessary to speak at such length about it. The only objection that can be raised against it is not: What did the Lord say? but: Did the Lord *mean* what He said? Our opponents concede: "Accepting the words in their literal sense, you Lutherans are in the right; but how can this be?" That is the highest laudation one can give a Lutheran: he abides by the Word. When Dr. Eck was asked, "Can you refute the Lutherans?" he replied, "With the church-fathers, yes; with Scripture, no." Then he was told by one of his own faith, "I see the Lutherans are entrenched within the Scriptures, and we are outside of them."

God grant that you to-day have again been confirmed in the belief "that these words: 'This is My body, this is My blood,' still hold good and true." Amen.

www.ingramcontent.com/pod-product-compliance
Lightning Source LLC
Chambersburg PA
CBHW030637150426
42813CB00050B/25

* 9 7 8 0 7 5 8 6 2 7 4 0 7 *